MODERN WORLD NATIONS

Spain

Zoran Pavlović
and Reuel Hanks
Oklahoma State University

Series Consulting Editor
Charles F. Gritzner
South Dakota State University

CHELSEA HOUSE
PUBLISHERS
An imprint of Infobase Publishing

Frontispiece: Flag of Spain

Cover: The Mezquita (Great Mosque) was built in Cordoba, Spain, in the tenth century, when Muslim Moors ruled the country. Today it is home to a Catholic church.

Spain

Copyright © 2006 by Infobase Publishing

Chelsea House
An imprint of Infobase Publishing
132 West 31st Street
New York NY 10001

Library of Congress Cataloging-in-Publication Data

Pavlovic, Zoran.
  Spain / Zoran Pavlovic and Reuel R. Hanks.
    p. cm. — (Modern world nations)
  Includes bibliographical references and index.
  ISBN 0-7910-6697-5 (hardcover)
  1. Spain—Juvenile literature. I. Hanks, Reuel R. II. Title. II. Series.
DF720.P38 2006
946—dc22   2006002218

Chelsea House books are available at special discounts when purchased in bulk quantities for businesses, associations, institutions, or sales promotions. Please call our Special Sales Department in New York at (212) 967-8800 or (800) 322-8755.

You can find Chelsea House on the World Wide Web at http://www.chelseahouse.com

Series and cover design by Takeshi Takahashi

Printed in the United States of America

Bang 21C 10 9 8 7 6 5 4 3 2 1

This book is printed on acid-free paper.

All links, web addresses, and Internet search terms were checked and verified to be correct at the time of publication. Because of the dynamic nature of the web, some addresses and links may have changed since publication and may no longer be valid.

Table of Contents

MODERN WORLD NATIONS

Spain

Introducing Spain

" **I**t is difficult not to like Spain, not to enjoy the atmosphere of such a civilized society, and not to admire the achievements of its people," noted *The Economist* in a recent survey of Spain. This is the attitude shared by so many who are familiar with this wonderful country and its people. Falling in love with Spain and Spaniards is predictable, understandable, and unquestionable. After visiting the country once, most travelers look forward to returning. Its magnificent landscapes and dynamic culture are an irresistible lure.

Spain is a kingdom in southwestern Europe, tucked between the Mediterranean Sea and the Atlantic Ocean. Together with Portugal, it occupies Iberia, a peninsula that is largely cut off from the rest of Europe by the rugged Pyrenees Mountains. Its isolation from Europe and proximity to northwest Africa have played a very important role in the country's culture and history. Although Spain's influential role in the historical development of most American nations, including the United States, is well known, few Americans really know Spain. Our knowledge of Spain and its culture generally does not extend beyond tourist-type facts, such as, "they speak Spanish and love soccer." In reality, culturally, the country is much more complex—a product of a rich history and the geographic location that helped in creating that complexity.

At one point in history, Spain was not only one of the world's most influential countries, but it was also the world's strongest empire, controlling vast areas and people of different cultures. It was from Spain's city of Cadiz that Christopher Columbus began his first voyage, sailing westward with the hope of reaching the Orient. Of course, he discovered the Americas, misnamed the native population (thinking he had reached the Indies), and began a race to acquire colonial land holdings and their wealth. Some scholars suggest that Columbus knew all along what he was doing, but it is doubtful that we will ever know for certain. What is known is that within a century of his landfall, Spanish conquistadors had conquered most of the New World. Spain's power was elevated for nearly three centuries by the gold, silver, and other riches that flowed into the homeland. This meteoric rise in Spanish power occurred just after its Christian forces finally defeated Muslim Moorish forces and liberated the Iberian Peninsula after seven centuries of occupation.

No glory lasts forever, and neither did Spain's. In more recent times, Spain experienced a dramatic decline in power, wealth, and culture. It also underwent a period of self-generated isolation, during the dictatorial reign of fascist strongman Francisco Franco. This period of stagnation lasted for decades; it followed the end of a bloody civil war in 1939. Fortunately, after Franco's death in 1975, the country rapidly transformed from a European backwater into a progressive, democratic, and open nation. Today's Spain is a far cry from the provincial society that a century earlier was rapidly falling behind industrialized West European countries such as the United Kingdom and Germany. The country now plays one of the more significant roles in the rapidly emerging European Union.

One of Spain's most valuable assets is its physical landscape, recognized for its beauty since the times of the Roman Empire. (Many influential Roman leaders, in fact, were actually born in present-day Spain, from where they eventually went to pillage other parts of Europe.) Its beaches today attract millions of visitors searching for their spot of paradise during both summer and winter seasons. Others explore the urban landscapes of Madrid, Barcelona, or Valencia or simply wander through picturesque countryside villages, studying the simple life. Tourism represents one of the most important sources of income to the Spanish economy.

MANY SPAINS

In terms of its peoples and their ways of life, Spain is by no means homogeneous. In fact, there are many Spains. Ethnic and linguistic differences among Spain's peoples often complicate the country's political situation. These differences generate separatist tendencies among some, who feel that their own ethnic identities may be endangered. This reaction is often quite common among ethnic groups. Tensions can arise when diverse ethnic groups share living space with one another. This is particularly true when some groups are perceived, for whatever reason, as being privileged. In Spain, for example, many Basques and Catalans believe that they are in an inferior position, particularly when compared to Castilians. Their political goals include unconditional territorial independence from Spain.

As is the case elsewhere in the world, people living in varied cultural environments react differently. One need travel no farther than the United States or Canada to realize the importance of regional identities. People living in Philadelphia rarely share life concerns of those living on a Montana ranch. Similarly, Madrid's urbanites believe that further development

Spain's beaches attract millions of tourists each year. Pictured here are beachgoers in Majorca (Mallorca), which is located in the Mediterranean Sea and the largest of Spain's Balearic Islands.

of the Spanish capital is far more significant for the country's future than slowly changing rural areas. Spaniards living in northwestern areas often share much different views on life than those living in northeast or southern regions. Contemporary Spain, therefore, is like a puzzle. The overall picture is really the sum of many pieces, each of which has its own distinct regional character and appearance.

In order to minimize regional differences and decentralize power in a country of this size, the government created smaller political units. The role of so-called autonomous communities is to provide a better quality of life to their residents. Local government, after all, is usually much more in touch with the needs and concerns of local people than is a distant national government. This is a big step from the fascistic iron fist that once controlled Spain.

These regional differences reflect Spain's unique heritage. Without understanding important cultural similarities and differences, it is not possible to comprehend a nation as a whole. A primary focus of this book is to take a close look at the different people and regions that come together to make Spain exceptional.

Most studies of geographic regions begin with a description of the natural environment. The land, climate, resources, and other natural elements form the foundation upon which cultures are built. People, after all, culturally adapt to, use, and modify the lands in which they live. Because of its importance, the introductory chapter of this book and others in the Modern World Nations series is followed by a chapter on physical geography.

CULTURE IS ALWAYS THE ANSWER

"What is where, why is it there, and why should we care?" are among the most important questions for geographers to answer. Why certain peoples and cultures are found in certain places is generally the result of decisions based on the relationship between people and the surrounding physical environment. Culture is humankind's adaptive mechanism. Humans adapt to the natural environment and use it to the best of their needs and technological abilities. This is why cultural landscapes of mountainous regions differ from those in lowlands. Compared to urban areas, the rural folk lifestyle unquestionably leaves a different impression. Dietary habits, religious beliefs, and other aspects of culture vary from place to place. Farmers residing in western Spain consume many foods that differ from those consumed by the residents of Valencia, in eastern Spain.

Of all aspects of culture, economics is perhaps the most important. A country's economic system and the economic well-being of its people influence nearly every other aspect of its culture. In Spain, the local economy developed differently in the coastal regions than it did inland, a reality that is clearly reflected on the landscape. The waters of the Atlantic Ocean and the Mediterranean Sea were rich in marine resources. These waters generously provided abundant foodstuffs to many generations of fishermen who looked to the sea as the primary provider of goods and economic success. When people utilize a particular environmental element for their own benefit, they then begin to rely on that particular resource. Seafaring people utilize the sea and are not afraid of it because their livelihood depends on this relationship. A visit to coastal towns provides an insight into this close relationship between culture and nature.

On the other hand—and this is where Spain is a rather interesting example of how culture works—the economic history of the country's heartland is much different from its coasts. Those Spaniards whose culture took advantage of inland mountains, plateaus, and plains practiced agriculture and cattle ranching as their primary economic activities. The existence of cultivated rolling hills, river valleys, and large areas of pasture-land contributed to the evolution of a unique way of life and cultural landscape.

This outlook was further underscored by the heartland's cultural isolation from the rest of Europe. Limited diffusion (cultural contact, hence the flow of culture traits, from the outside) was slow to reach and alter lifestyles in the interior. Society there remained socially stratified and culturally rigid. Change was slow in coming and was often met with great resistance. Such conditions generally result in social and cultural conformity, with people being reluctant to accept change, particularly those resulting from "foreign" contacts. They consider their own way of life superior to those of other cultures. This attitude, of course, can be a shortcoming. People who isolate themselves from outside ideas and material traits often

In mountainous regions, such as the northern Spanish principality of Asturias, the economy is much different from that of the country's coastal regions. The production of steel and coal mining have traditionally been the backbone of Asturias's economy, while its neighbor to the west, Galicia, relies heavily on fishing and agriculture.

remain provincial; that is, their culture fails to keep pace with the development of other cultures.

Eventually, however, Spain did change, and it is important that we understand how this came about. Perhaps it began with medieval unification, resulting from the marriage between Queen Isabella of Castile and King Ferdinand of Aragon in 1469. Simultaneously, Spain began to liberate the Iberian Peninsula from Muslim control that had been a force for some seven centuries. Castile and Aragon were the lands of interior people. Military *reconquista* (reconquest) stimulated cultural expansion. With the rest of the Iberian Peninsula under the firm control of Castile, the interior rural culture triumphed over others. With Christopher Columbus's help, this culture soon expanded even farther, ultimately occupying much of the Western Hemisphere. The conquest resulted in the claiming of lands and resources and the subjugation of many local cultures. This expansion and resulting exploitation established the foundation upon which Spain would build for several centuries.

Many complex questions relating to various aspects of Spain's past can be answered only by understanding the history of the country's culture. The success of twentieth-century fascism, for example, is one of those questions. How could Spain fall under the tightfisted rule of such a regime and remain under its control for decades? It requires a specific cultural setting for a nation to accept fascist rule over a long period of time. Why was Spain unable to prevent the loss of Latin American possessions, including Mexico, its crown jewel? How did it suddenly fall into the black hole of peripheral influence within Europe? What were the factors that eventually helped Spain overcome this enormous obstacle? What will the future bring? These are just some of the questions that can best be answered by thoughtfully considering the country's history and cultural geography. Each of these topics is discussed in the following chapters.

Today, an attention-grabbing cultural struggle exists in Spain. Throughout even the most remote areas of the country, folk cultures, with their traditional lifestyles, are vanishing. Popular culture, featuring urban life, a cash economy, and rapid change, is quickly reshaping Spanish society. At both the individual and group levels of society, people are demanding greater freedom and more civil rights. Spain may have become a victim of its own success. Castile's cultural dominance over other regions was once believed to be a cohesive and unifying force. Today, however, it is often seen as a destructive force that excludes various ethnic groups and drives a wedge between different peoples.

CHANGING TIMES

In a country that until recently was known as a bastion of socially conservative Catholicism, more liberal beliefs are beginning to take root. For example, during recent years, laws have been passed expanding individual rights for speedy divorces and allowing same-sex marriages. Both decisions are a direct blow not only to Catholicism, but to a society in which the concept of *machismo* (male dominance) originated. At the same time, Spain is also experiencing difficulties with low population growth, a problem shared by most postindustrial countries. Low rates of natural population increase present many problems in Western Europe today, particularly as it relates to immigration. Spain is one of many countries searching for the best solution for its growing immigrant population, which is predominantly from North Africa.

During recent decades, the global geographical-political situation has undergone significant changes, particularly in the area of antiterrorism. The growing threat of terrorism tragically struck at the heart of Spain in 2004. Just a few days before general elections, Madrid became the site of one of the most devastating terrorist attacks in European history. One of the results of this attack was that a new governing party, the Spanish Socialist-Workers Party, took control of the Spanish government. Chapter 5 explains many of the complex factors that influence a country's internal political conditions in today's complex and often turbulent world. Those times when a particular country could exist in cultural isolation from the rest of the world are long past. Today, we are all part of an interdependent global community and can be affected by events occurring in other parts of the globe. Spain also has its share of internal political conflicts at the regional level, however. For many years, Spain has been involved in domestic political disputes and struggles against its own home-grown terrorism. Future prospects for political balance that may satisfy all sides are also discussed in the proper context.

Experience has shown that perhaps the best way to avoid the disruption of destructive forces is to develop and expand a country's economy. When people are satisfied with their living conditions, they are less apt to become antagonistic, even if they are ethnically divided. Poor economic conditions often contribute to social and political turmoil and strife. Chapter 6 takes a look at Spain's current economic conditions. Topics discussed include the country's role in the European Union, its place in the world economic system, and transformations that can be expected in the future.

As you can see, this book is not a collection of several unrelated chapters. Rather, each chapter contributes to an integrated view of the "big picture" of Spain. This is the beauty of geography and the unique perspective that it contributes to furthering our understanding of the world. Geographers first analyze different topics in order to understand the background issues. Their emphasis, of course, is on the importance of location: what conditions are where, why are they located in a particular place or places, and why are they important? This is the first stage of geographers' work. In the second stage, they create a synthesis of individual findings in order to discover the big picture. To understand present conditions, geographers always look to the past. In this case, an understanding of Spain's cultural history is essential if we are to understand how the country's social, political, and economic patterns have emerged. This knowledge also helps us better forecast the country's future.

In the final chapter, we will take a look into the crystal ball, to attempt to predict Spain's future. The geography of the future is frequently a domain of imagination, simply because imagination is so often used in prediction. Obviously, no one can be certain of the exact pathway a country and its people will follow in the future. It was once suggested that nothing represents the country of Spain better than its wines. Perhaps that is an excellent analogy, considering the great importance of wine in Spanish society. Grapes have been grown in the country for thousands of years. The wines they produce are bold and strong in flavor and made from vines growing under difficult environmental conditions. Grapes are domestic and unrefined. Tradition in Spanish winemaking is so deeply rooted that because of its lack of modernization, it cannot compete on an international level. Laws are designed to rigidly protect tradition, preserve the status quo, and block the outside influence of global trends, because of the fear of change.

However, if grape growers changed their attitude and society supported them, Spain could produce some of the world's finest wines. All that is needed is to transform everyone's way of thinking and change the existing cultural system. Spain, just like its winemakers, is standing at the crossroad of a globalized world—with two choices. One is to take a route that will lead the country to becoming a leader among the world's communities. The other pathway leads to a continuation of the search for identity, while preserving deeply entrenched traditions. After reading this book, the authors hope that you will have a much clearer picture of the direction Spain, its people, and its culture will take.

Physical
Landscapes

S pain offers a splendid example of why location and physical geographic conditions are important to the culture of a people. Until the sixteenth century, the Iberian Peninsula was little more than a remote outpost, of very little economic or other importance. Its location was a hindrance. Lying south of the towering Pyrenees and at the western end of the Mediterranean Sea, which had long been dominated by Phoenicians, Egyptians, Greeks, and Romans, Spain's location was peripheral to the rest of Europe. This would all change, though, as a result of the Iberian Voyages of Discovery. From an isolated cultural "backwater," Spain and Portugal were about to become Europe's focal point of power and influence.

What changed was culture—in the form of navigational technology, ships, geographical knowledge, and a worldview that was rapidly changing from "inward" to "outward." Beginning with

Columbus's epic voyage in 1492, explorers discovered the New World and transoceanic travel developed rapidly. These developments caused a major shift in power and influence, not only in Europe, but globally, as well. The pendulum of political and economic importance shifted from the Mediterranean Sea to the Atlantic Ocean. No longer outliers, Spain and Portugal now occupied what had become Europe's most important location. It held this position for about three centuries, until another change in technology (the steam engine) eventually caused the pendulum to shift toward northwestern Europe.

Geographers always emphasize the importance of location. Just as historians are concerned with events in time, geographers focus on conditions of place. We can learn much about a particular country simply by understanding the significance of its position on Earth's surface. This holds true for a country's physical geographic conditions, as well as its cultural characteristics. For example, because Spain is located on a peninsula, it exhibits a number of climatic characteristics unique to marine environments.

THE IMPORTANCE OF LOCATION

Spain is one of two countries located in the extreme southwestern section of the European continent, a region known as the Iberian Peninsula. Except for the boundary with its smaller neighbor, Portugal, Spain is divided from other neighboring countries by substantial natural barriers. It directly borders only one major country, France (Andorra, a small democracy that is only about two-and-a-half times the size of Washington, D.C., lies between France and Spain). Most of this barrier is made up of large bodies of water—the Mediterranean Sea and the Atlantic Ocean. Even though a substantial amount of Spanish territory borders the Atlantic, geographers almost always refer to this country as belonging to the Mediterranean region. This is because of the strong

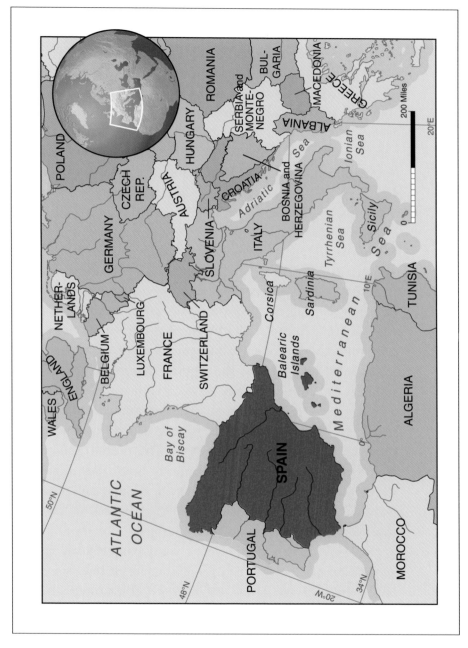

Spain is located in the southwestern corner of Europe and shares the Iberian Peninsula with Portugal. Spain is slightly more than twice the size of the state of Oregon and the third-largest nation in Europe.

cultural and historical ties that both Spain and Portugal (itself lacking a direct physical connection with the Mediterranean) share with other southern European nations.

Were it not for the Christian reconquista—the expulsion of Islamic African Moors from Spain by Christian rulers—and the narrow Strait of Gibraltar, Spain could have been closer to North Africa than to Europe, not only spatially, but culturally, as well. This 8-mile- (14-kilometer-) wide strait divides two continents and two major cultural regions. To the north, Spain and France share a boundary that stretches from the lowlands of Catalonian beaches westward through the high-rising Pyrenees Mountains. It eventually reaches the shores of the Bay of Biscay in northern Spain's Basque homeland. Mountains can play a positive role in connecting places if they have something to offer, such as pastures, water, or wide passages serving as transportation routes. Alpine Europe offers a good example. The Pyrenees, on the other hand, were fairly dry, largely impenetrable, and in other ways considered undesirable by people of the region. They served as an ideal political and cultural barrier between France and Spain and as a refuge area (for Andorrans). The mountains offered little productive land, a factor that also lessened any interest in them as a location for settlement. The border and region have rarely been contested by France or Spain, although they have been the setting of military invasions, on occasion. Nowadays, however, invasions are from hordes of tourists, most of whom are from northern Europe.

Colonial expansion played a significant role in Spain's acquisition of several territories disconnected from the mainland. The Canary Islands, off the west coast of Africa, and several small possessions near Morocco, are remnants of Spanish colonialism. In the Mediterranean Sea, Spanish territorial reach extends to the Balearic Islands (off the coast of Valencia), which have a long history of Iberian presence. One odd remnant of Europe's checkered political past is the small

Spanish exclave of Llivia. This small town and its 1,200 inhabitants lie tucked away in the French Pyrenees about 12 miles
(20 kilometers) east of Andorra and less than one mile from
the Spanish border.

Spain has long benefited from its location and ready access
to the sea. Many European countries are much less fortunate,
including some that are completely landlocked. In addition, the
shortest, fastest, and least expensive route between Europe and
North Africa (a place of considerable economic importance to
the European Union) leads across Spanish territory.

THE LAND

Spain's cultural ecology—the way humans adapt to, use,
and modify the natural environment in which they live—
represents a wonderful example of cultural adaptation in a
not particularly welcoming land. Present-day cultural landscapes are gradually losing the visible evidence of the harsh
realities faced in earlier times. Likewise, modern technology
has helped lessen the impact of the difficult environmental
challenges imposed on residents of the Iberian Peninsula. The
landscape is made up of a combination of landforms, with
few water features.

Mountains and rugged plateaus cover a substantial amount
of Spain's territory. This landscape not only influences the
physical landscape but also the region's climate, vegetation, and
other physical conditions. Land features, of course, pose both
obstacles to and opportunities for human use. In addition,
people living in mountainous regions tend to be more independent and show sharper regional cultural differences. These
conditions, of course, are the result of the isolation created by
rugged terrain.

The largest mountain range in terms of area is the Pyrenees,
located in the extreme northeastern part of the country. Here,
the highest peaks exceed 11,000 feet (3,350 meters), just slightly
lower than the highest volcanic peaks in the Sierra Nevada of

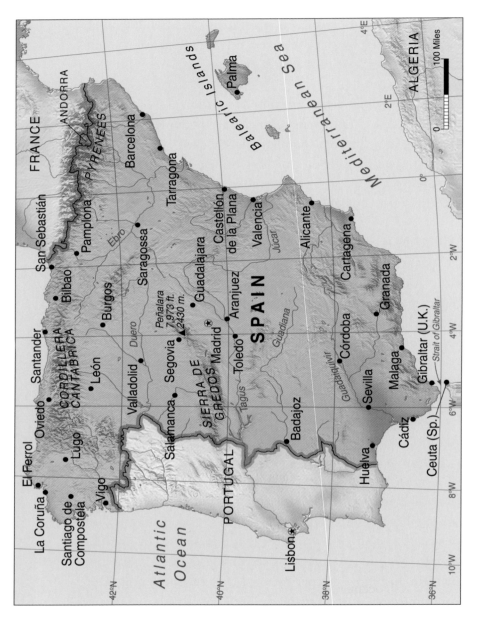

Spain's topography is primarily made up of a large plateau, bordered by rugged hills and mountains in the north and central part of the country. The nation's most prominent geographical feature is the Pyrenees Mountain range in northeastern Spain. The Pyrenees form a 270-mile (430-kilometer) boundary between Spain and France, from the Mediterranean Sea to the Bay of Biscay.

southern Spain. Local terrain in the Pyrenees is a sequence of high peaks, narrow valleys, and rapidly flowing streams carving narrow canyons. At the highest elevation, alpine glaciers are still present, although they are melting away with the warmer temperatures of recent decades. Extending westward from the Pyrenees is a much lower range, the Cordillera Cantabrica. Its highest peaks are several thousand feet lower than those of the Pyrenees, making the range less of a barrier. This range did, however, play a significant historical role in helping form strong regional identities in central and northwestern Spain.

In Galicia and elsewhere in coastal northwestern Spain, people were drawn to the sea and its varied maritime resources. Inland, on the central plateaus, people generally practiced various agriculture-related activities. Because of the difficult terrain and general remoteness from the rest of Spain, these northern mountainous areas have experienced considerable emigration (movement out of the area). The young, particularly, have been leaving the region in search of better social and economic opportunities.

Two more major mountain ranges extend across the heart of Spain—Sistema Central and Sistema Ibérico. These highlands, recognized by various local names, surround Madrid, Spain's capital and fastest-growing city. The Cordillera Penibetica in the province of Andalucía is southern Spain's equivalent to the northern mountains. Although smaller in area than their northern counterparts, these highlands are among Europe's best known for several reasons. Historically, during the Moorish occupation of Iberia, these mountains were in the center of the kingdom. The fabulous city of Granada is located on the slopes of the Sierra Nevada here. Here, too, is Europe's southernmost ski center, with runs plunging down the slopes of snow-covered peaks overlooking the nearby Mediterranean coast. Mainland Spain's highest peak, Mulhacén, towers 11,423 feet (3,482 meters) above the surrounding countryside. (The country's highest mountain is Pico de Teide, on Tenerife in the Canary Islands, which reaches an elevation of 12,198 feet, or 3,718 meters.)

Except in the northwest, where they rise from the sea, Spain's mountains generally parallel the coast. As a result, Spain's coasts are relatively unspectacular. On the other hand, this physical condition has contributed to the formation of thousands of beaches. From its border with France, and all the way to its border with Portugal and along both coasts, the country has some of Europe's most popular coastal tourist destinations.

Even though mountain and coastal features are Spain's best-known and most spectacular natural features, rocky plateaus and rolling hills are the country's most common landscapes. In all of Europe, only Switzerland has a higher average elevation than Spain. This relief has resulted from the collision of the African and European tectonic plates. The geologic clash lifted portions of Europe, creating mountains and high plateaus. In Spain, only a small portion of the country lies at an elevation below 1,500 feet (460 meters).

WEATHER AND CLIMATE

Weather is a current atmospheric condition, whereas *climate* is the long-term average of weather conditions. Climatologists (scientists who study climate) use the long-term information to create charts and maps that show geographic areas with specific climatic conditions. Some countries may have only one climatic zone, whereas others (such as the United States) have many. Understanding climatic data is quite important geo-graphically because weather and climate often play a key role in the evolution of both natural and cultural landscapes. Through the process of cultural adaptation, people "adjust" themselves to the surrounding environment. They develop adequate technology, human skills, and economic practices in order to survive and, hopefully, prosper. This is why when people

The Sierra Nevada, in southern Spain, are home to Europe's southernmost ski resorts. From the top of the mountain range's highest peak, Veleta, skiers can see across the Mediterranean to the Atlas Mountains of Morocco.

migrate, they often move to places with a similar climate and economic potential, because this allows them to use their acquired knowledge and skills.

In Spain, the climate is relatively dry, and crop yields are generally low. As a result, the primary agricultural activity is grazing—cattle ranching and sheep herding. Cattle ranching has been practiced in Iberia for at least 2,000 years, and Iberian Basques have a long and honored tradition of working as shepherds. Later, when many Spaniards moved to the New World, they continued these traditional activities in similar climatic conditions in the American southwest and throughout much of Latin America.

Spain is influenced by two major climate types. A Mediterranean climate dominates in the central and eastern regions, and an oceanic climate in the northern and northwestern regions. Worldwide, both climates are present in the middle latitudes (roughly 30 to 60 degrees north of the equator). The Mediterranean is quite unique because it is the only climate that experiences a pronounced summer drought. Nearly all precipitation in this climatic region falls during the winter months. It is, of course, named after the geographic region where it occurs, around much of the Mediterranean Sea. In Europe, that zone stretches from Turkey to Portugal. The American equivalent would be the climate of coastal Southern California.

The Mediterranean climate extends across most of the country, except in the far north and a small area of the southeast. Because of its closeness to the sea, Spain enjoys moderate temperatures and adequate precipitation. In fact, conditions are so pleasant that most people believe that the Mediterranean is the most enjoyable climate in the world in which to live. Winters are mild and moist. Most precipitation falls in the form of rain, which accompanies winter Atlantic air masses that penetrate the peninsula from the west. When snow does occur, it melts away rapidly, except at high elevations. Temperatures rarely fall below freezing, except in mountainous regions. During the winter, most of the country experiences temperatures averaging 40° to 60°F (5°–15°C). Summers are warm and dry. Coastal temperatures rarely rise above the 80s (27°–35°C). In the interior, far removed from the cooling influence of the sea, daily temperature averages may climb into the 80s (20s C). Occasionally, in the interior, summer temperatures can reach 100° (40°C). Because the air is dry, however, these warmer temperatures are not extremely uncomfortable.

Short and sometimes violent storms are the main form of summer precipitation in the Mediterranean climate. In many places, moisture is insufficient to support dry farming (raising crops without irrigation) and stream flow is not adequate to support irrigation. Other than in some mountainous areas, forests are rare in Spain. Shrub, bush, and grassland vegetation is the most common plant cover. A lack of adequate moisture is one natural condition to which people had to culturally adapt if they were to thrive in this environment. As a result, Spain is a well-known producer of such drought-resistant crops as olives (oil), grapes (wine), and various fruits that are acclimated to such conditions. Another pleasant characteristic of the Mediterranean climate is the high number of sunny days experienced throughout the year. Sunlight, of course, is ideal for the growing of fruit and other crops.

Marine West Coast is Spain's other major climate. In the United States, this climate occurs along the coasts of northern California, Oregon, and Washington. Its main characteristic is precipitation fairly equally distributed throughout the year, high humidity, frequent cloud cover, and a lack of extreme temperatures. Snow falls only in higher elevations. This climate is strongly influenced by air masses that move eastward from across the Atlantic Ocean, throughout nearly all of the year. This air is saturated with moisture, which falls in the form of light and constant rain, rather than as thunderstorms. Constant drizzle contributes to a rather bleak landscape, particularly during the fall and winter months. Residents adapt, though, finding the weather to be a wonderful excuse for a game of chess or a discussion about their favorite soccer team!

Very small areas experience climatic conditions not discussed above. These are usually places in which precipitation is unusually low in winter months—locations where physical barriers limit the penetration of moisture-bearing westerly winds and Atlantic air masses. In the late autumn, when winds shift direction from the southeast to the northeast, some areas in Spain fall into the rain shadow. East of Cordillera Penibetica is a small area that best illustrates this climatic condition. Here, winters are much drier than elsewhere in southern Spain.

HYDROGEOGRAPHY

Spain, unlike many other midlatitude countries, suffers from a critical shortage of freshwater resources. In many ways, it resembles the state of Nevada in that it lacks large lakes and long rivers. Only one river, the Tajo, is more than 600 miles (965 kilometers) long. Other major rivers are the Guadalquivir, Ebro, Guadiana, and Duero. A rather interesting fact is that the Ebro is the only major Spanish river that flows into the Mediterranean Sea rather than the Atlantic Ocean.

Most of Spain's rivers flow westward into the Atlantic because of the east-to-west downward slope of the land. This reality has contributed to an uneven distribution of fresh-water resources: Eastern Spain has much less surface water than the western part of the country. As the rivers flow westward, they create broad alluvial (water-deposited sediments) plains and marshlands, both of which are desirable in this type of environment. The best such example is the broad Andalucían Plain formed by the Rio Guadalquivir inland from its mouth in the Gulf of Cadiz. This region has a long and impressive history of settlement and agriculture, dating to ancient times. Two important Spanish cities, Seville and Cordoba, are located on this fertile plain.

Most rivers are quite short and ill suited to navigation. Many of the streams depend on spring and summer mountain snowmelt or, in the Mediterranean climate region, on winter rains. By summer, many of the riverbeds are dry, leaving the lands through which they flow parched. Some streams flow across areas of karst topography (dominated by limestone). Because limestone is so porous, streams frequently disappear into the ground, flow beneath the surface for some distance, and then reappear elsewhere.

Considering the country's size, surprisingly few large natural lakes exist. Most lakes are of glacial (mountain lakes) or karst (sinkhole) origin. During dry years, many lakes and ponds temporarily cease to exist. Later, with an increase in groundwater levels, snowmelt, and recharge from rivers, they reappear. The largest bodies of fresh water are the human-made reservoirs (artificial lakes) formed behind dams. Reservoirs serve multiple purposes: They are harnessed to create hydroelectric energy, their water can be used for irrigation and domestic purposes, and they are wonderful recreational sites.

NATURAL HAZARDS AND ENVIRONMENTAL ISSUES

One unfortunate aspect of the Mediterranean climate is frequent occurrence of wildfires during its long periods of summer drought. As happens each summer in Southern California, dry conditions contribute to a high fire risk in vegetation dominated by scrub bushes, shrubs, and dried grasses. These plants are adapted to summer aridity, and, in fact, summer is the period of plant dormancy in the Mediterranean climate! As the summer progresses, plants become increasingly dry, and even a cigarette can generate a huge and devastating inferno. Fires not only damage the land, they also put people in grave danger, forcing evacuations and often destroying entire settlements. Surprisingly, many Mediterranean plants are pyrophytic (fire dependent) and actually depend upon fire to reproduce and thrive.

Today, nearly all fires are caused by human negligence rather than by lightning or some other natural cause. Weed burning, campfires left unattended, careless tourists, and people throwing lit cigarettes are among the causes of wildfires, which are Spain's major environmental hazard. Although political authorities designated substantial funding to protect the country from wildfires, this protection has been extremely difficult to implement. In addition to accidental fires, another form of fire-related damage is happening with increasing frequency. Today, some fires are deliberately set for the purpose of disrupting daily life and economic activity. Although such fires are very easy and inexpensive to start, the results can be

Wildfires are Spain's predominant environmental hazard, and during the summer of 2005, thousands of fires, including 22 designated as major fires, were reported. Pictured here is a firefighter in Ourense, in the north-western province of Galicia, during the outbreak in 2005.

devastating. This form of terrorism is causing Spanish officials deep concern.

Spain also faces the threat of two other natural hazards: earthquakes and volcanic eruptions. Although the country is located in an earthquake-prone zone, which stretches across southern Europe, Spain is blessed by having had very few devastating seismic events. This does not mean, however, that numerous earthquakes of smaller magnitude do not occur. They are quite common and often cause some minor damage. No one knows, however, when the Big One will hit. For most of the Iberian Peninsula, it is just a matter of time.

Earthquakes and volcanoes both occur in areas of geologic instability, such as along the edge of tectonic plates. Mainland Spain is relatively fortunate in having little volcanic activity.

The Canary Islands, however, are of volcanic origin and during recent geologic history have been quite active. In recent years, some scientists have become deeply concerned over what could be an eruption of unparalleled devastation on the island of La Palma. Although this event may be hundreds or even thousands of years in the future, many geologists are convinced that it will occur and are beginning to sound the alarm. A violent eruption, they argue, would send a huge portion of the island sliding into the Atlantic Ocean. The resulting displacement of water would create a huge tsunami (tidal wave) that would sweep across the Atlantic Basin and beyond. Although it would take some time to reach the mainland of Europe, Africa, and the Americas, devastation would be unparalleled. Millions of lives could be lost, entire coastal cities could be washed away, and trillions of dollars of property could be lost forever. Before you begin worrying, however, other seismologists (scientists studying earthquakes) are not convinced that this scenario is impending and, in fact, are quite sure that it will not happen.

As experience has amply shown, only an affluent society can afford the luxury of a clean and protected environment. During recent decades, Spain has experienced widespread prosperity. This is reflected in a growing recognition of the importance of environmental preservation. There is a substantial increase in both funding made available and the number of areas that have been protected. Wealth, on the other hand, can generate some problems. More leisure time and money to spend, for example, means greater use of and damage to Spain's beautiful coasts. In fact, coastal zone and beach environments have experienced serious degradation. Also, because of increased industrialization, Spain's rapidly expanding settlements are dealing with environmental pollution and the loss of agricultural land to urban sprawl.

3

Spain
Through Time

Much of Spain's historical geography is a record of the movement of peoples motivated by migration, invasion, or trade. In this regard, Iberia's position has played an important role. The peninsula bends downward from western Europe toward North Africa, with the southern tip of the Spanish mainland almost touching Africa, its neighbor to the south. As a result, Spain lies astride two vital avenues of movement. These crucial routes provided the region with a dual strategic importance from its earliest history. The first avenue runs north and south, ensuring that Spain would serve as the bridge, both literally and figuratively, between Africa and Europe. The second route lies along Spain's southern coast, through the narrow Strait of Gibraltar, which allows access between the Mediterranean Sea and the Atlantic Ocean. Due to the country's strategic location, migration, invasion, and trade all became themes of Spanish historical geography.

EARLY INFLUENCES ON SPANISH HISTORICAL GEOGRAPHY

The first people to move onto the territory of Iberia were probably the Basques. Their origins are obscure, although they appear to have settled the region of northern Spain by the Neolithic era (10,000 to 12,000 B.C.), if not before. Around 1,500 B.C., the Iberian people arrived. They probably migrated across the narrow strait between Africa and southern Spain, establishing a route that would be followed by numerous invaders in later centuries. By the beginning of the first millennium B.C., these groups were joined in the region by the great trading and colonizing peoples of the ancient world, the Phoenicians and Greeks. Both groups arrived by sea to trade. Ultimately, they established port settlements along the coast of southern Spain. The Phoenicians built most of their ports along the coast of present-day Andalucía, Spain's southernmost province. The Greeks, who appeared several centuries after the Phoenicians, established a presence in the eastern regions of Catalonia and Valencia. The Greeks brought two crops that would become synonymous with the Spanish countryside: olives and grapes. Even today, more than 2,000 years later, these products are an important Spanish crop. Greek colonists in Spain were exporting wine to other Greek settlements as early as 500 B.C.

Additional cultural influences appeared over the next several centuries. Migrating Celtic peoples crossed central Europe and flowed into northern Iberia. They were followed soon afterward by invaders from the sea. First, by water, came armies from Carthage, including those of the famous Hannibal; later came legions from that great general's archenemy, Rome. The cultural and historical imprint of the Romans can still be observed across the landscape of Spain. There are, for example, the ruins of massive aqueducts, roadways (some still in use today), and key fortified cities such as Toledo, Tarragona, and Barcelona. Even the modern name of the

The Romans first came to Spain in the second century B.C., and would later annex the region during the reign of Augustus Caesar. During their time in the province of Hispania, the Romans built aqueducts to transport water from nearby rivers to towns. Pictured here is the Roman aqueduct at Segovia, which was built circa A.D. 52 and was used to move water from the Frio River, 18 kilometers away.

country is a remnant of Roman rule. *Hispania* was the province's toponym (place name) in Latin, rendered today as *España* in Spanish, a language derived from Latin.

Roman rule not only transformed the region's physical landscape, but the cultural landscape as well. Two enduring cultural features were introduced into Iberia during the half millennium of the *Pax Romana* (era of Roman rule, 27 B.C. to A.D. 476)—Latin and Christianity. Latin served as the basis for both Castilian Spanish, the region's primary language, and Catalan, spoken today by about 6 million people in eastern Spain. Christian missionaries appeared in Iberia during the first century of Christianity, and the faith had gained widespread acceptance by A.D. 300. A Christian shrine of great importance during the Middle Ages is located at Compostela, in northern Spain. Here, according to legend, the cathedral at Santiago de Compostela houses the relics of Saint James, one of the Twelve Apostles. The site has attracted millions of visitors from throughout the Christian world for more than 1,000 years. In the centuries following the Roman collapse around A.D. 450, Christianity became firmly established as a central element of Spanish identity. The region's cultural landscape amply attests the importance of religion to the Spanish people. There are thousands of churches, monasteries, and shrines scattered throughout the country.

The centuries following the decline of Rome would bring still more migrants and invaders who would shape Spanish geography. Germanic tribes from central Europe, including the Vandals, briefly pushed into the region. The Visigoths, a Germanic tribe who had become allies of the Romans, also crossed into Iberia from neighboring Gaul (France). The kingdom established by this new Germanic aristocracy was plagued by instability and intrigue for two centuries. Ongoing conflict opened the way for yet another wave of newcomers who would have an indelible impact on Spanish historical geography.

THE EMERGENCE OF MUSLIM SPAIN

In A.D. 570, an event occurred thousands of miles from Spain that would profoundly shape the country's cultural identity and geography and, indeed, that of the entire world. In that year, an Arabian trader named Muhammad was born. He would soon emerge as the Prophet of God (*Allah* in Arabic) to the followers of the new faith he founded, Islam. In the century after his death, followers of Islam moved out of Arabia to spread their faith. By the early eighth century, they had traveled across North Africa. In 711, Muslim forces crossed the Strait of Gibraltar and penetrated the Iberian Peninsula, easily overwhelming the disorganized and demoralized armies of the Visigoths. The Muslims, composed mostly of Arabs and Berbers, quickly brought most of Spain under their control. Afterward, they continued to drive northeastward. Finally, in 732, their expansion was halted by the army of Charles Martel, at Tours, in western France. The Muslims would penetrate no farther into western Europe. But they had conquered nearly all of Iberia, a land they dubbed *al-Andalus*, or "land of the Vandals" in Arabic. Only a narrow strip of territory in northern Spain remained under the rule of Christian princes. The stage was set for an enduring struggle between two faiths that would later culminate in a series of Catholic crusades designed to wrest control of the Holy Land from the Muslims.

Islamic culture would leave an indelible mark on Spain, an imprint still evident nearly 500 years after the last Muslim rulers left the country. The magnificent contributions of the "Moors," as the Muslims were called, are epitomized in one of the most beautiful buildings in Europe—the spectacular Alhambra Palace, in Granada. Indeed, the civilization established by Spain's Muslim masters in the centuries immediately after their arrival eclipsed any other in Europe at the time. As was the case with Islam itself, events in far-off Arabia would have a dramatic effect on Spain's historical development in the years after the arrival of the Muslims.

Muhammad died in the Arabian city of Medina in 632. Following his death, a powerful clan called the Umayyads controlled the office of *caliph*, the official who was both the supreme religious and the secular leader of the Muslim community. In 750, a rival clan, the Abbasids, swept the Umayyads from power and established a new dynasty, destroying most of the extended Umayyad family in the process. One Umayyad prince managed to escape the bloody wrath of his rivals, however, and eventually made his way with a small party of followers to the Strait of Gibraltar. This man was Abd al-Rahman. When al-Rahman crossed to the Spanish side of the Strait in 754, the Islamic lands in Spain were in political disarray. The prince took little time to amass an army and take the city of Cordoba, making it his capital. Thus began one of the most enlightened, cosmopolitan, and tolerant societies in history.

Umayyad rule of Cordoba lasted for nearly 300 years. During this period, the city was dominated by Muslims, but Christians and Jews were tolerated and fared well under Islamic rule. Cordoba became one of the largest cities in Europe and featured pleasant parks, gardens, and fountains, along with a university that attracted students from both the Islamic world and Christian Europe. Muslim rulers improved the region's irrigation systems and planted new crops, especially citrus fruits and rice. In 929, one of al-Rahman's descendants, Abd al-Rahman III, declared himself caliph, challenging the authority of the Abbasid caliphate in Baghdad. His rule represented the high point of Islamic culture in Spain, but his death in 1031 initiated a long, slow retreat of Muslim domination there.

Spain's remaining Christian territories attempted to regain land almost from the moment of Muslim conquest. This was a centuries-long process known to modern Spaniards as the reconquista. It was not a steady, consistent campaign. In fact, more than 700 years were required to push the Muslims out of Iberia. The lines marking the Muslim and Christian domains frequently shifted, and sometimes Muslim and Christian principalities combined to fight a common foe. Many legendary figures lived and fought during this era of Spanish history, most notably *El Cid*, a Christian warrior who served both Christian and Muslim rulers.

The reconquista ended in 1492, when the last Muslim kingdoms in Spain were eliminated. The rulers who oversaw this fundamental change were Ferdinand of Aragon and Isabella of Castile, who would quickly emerge as Europe's most powerful monarchs. This husband and wife duo would launch an Italian explorer, Christopher Columbus, toward the west and with him the entire Age of Discovery. At the same time, they would oversee the beginning of the infamous Spanish Inquisition, a campaign of torture and abuse directed at Jews and Muslims who remained in Christian-dominated Spain. Less than 50 years after the reconquista, Spain had emerged as a leading global power, constructing a massive empire that stretched from Florida to the Philippines and southwestern Canada to the southern tip of South America. The Spanish empire was truly the first world power and left a lasting mark on global cultural geography.

THE RISE AND FALL OF IMPERIAL SPAIN

The expansion of the Spanish empire between 1492 and 1600 spread Spanish culture to millions of people and fundamentally shaped the cultural history of the New World. Spain acquired enormous stretches of new land in South and Central America, as well as in the Caribbean, and smaller holdings in Africa and the Pacific Basin. This great cultural eruption from the European continent stands second only to a similar expansion, a century later, of English culture, to every corner of the globe. As a result, Spanish is currently the first language of more than 330 million people—but only about 40 million people live in Spain today!

The decline of Spanish imperial fortunes may be traced to a single event, although the complete decline of the empire took several centuries. The event that turned the tide was a decisive naval battle—the defeat of the famous Spanish Armada by Great Britain in 1588. After this loss, the British would rapidly displace first the Spanish and then the Dutch as the world's leading seafaring nation. Over the next 150 years, Spain lost much territory in Europe, although it maintained a vast overseas empire. The War of Spanish Succession in the early 1700s resulted in significant losses of Spanish land in Europe, including Gibraltar to the British. Napoleon's invasion of Spain a century later signaled the complete collapse of a country that had once been Europe's most powerful state. Spain emerged from the struggles of the Napoleonic era weakened and in turmoil. Within three decades, it had lost virtually all of its colonial holdings in the New World. This was not only damaging to the country's prestige, but it had a crippling effect on the economy. Over the next century, broad divisions would open in Spanish society between rich and poor, urban and rural, and church and state. To compound the country's challenges, some regions, especially the Basque lands and Catalonia, showed an increased desire to break free from control of the Spanish Crown. Spanish weakness was punctuated at the conclusion of the 1800s. By 1898, most of Spain's remaining colonies, including the Philippines, Cuba, and Puerto Rico, were lost as a result of the Spanish-American War.

THE FRANCO DICTATORSHIP

During the early decades of the twentieth century, the political and social instability that plagued Spain throughout the nineteenth century took on new dimensions. The Spanish political scene became increasingly polarized between those on the right and left, as governments from both ends of the political spectrum failed to bring stability to the country. By the 1930s, the country was ripe for civil war. In 1936, General Francisco Franco led a revolt against the Spanish government, starting in Morocco, then crossing the Strait of Gibraltar into mainland Spain. The war raged for three devastating years, and in the end Franco and his Falange Party controlled Spain. The Spanish Civil War, memorialized in Ernest Hemingway's *For Whom the Bell Tolls,* was a brutal conflict that drew in many outside forces, including soldiers and weapons from Italy, Germany, and the Soviet Union. Ultimately, some 350,000 Spaniards perished in the war, and the country suffered widespread destruction.

Franco moved swiftly to construct a dictatorship, severely limiting political and social liberties. Although supported by Nazi Germany's Adolf Hitler during the civil war, Franco shrewdly maintained Spain's neutrality during World War II.

During the Spanish Civil War (1936 to 1939), nationalist forces under the command of General Francisco Franco overthrew the Second Spanish Republic, which had ruled Spain since 1931. After the war, Franco would serve as *Jefe del Estado*, or Head of State, until his death in 1975.

Spain remained something of an outcast in the postwar era, though, and was not allowed to join the United Nations until 1955. Although Franco was inhuman and would not tolerate political dissent, he was successful at improving the country's economy, which attracted both foreign aid and large numbers of tourists. At the same time, support for independence among many of the Basques increased, resulting in a violent campaign of bombings and assassinations in the last two decades of Franco's rule.

DEMOCRACY RETURNS

Franco's death in 1975 signaled the return of Spain to the European mainstream. The young Spanish king Juan Carlos swiftly steered the country toward democracy, implementing political, social, and economic reforms. By 1986, the Spanish economy had improved to such an extent that Spain was allowed to join the European Economic Community (EEC), the forerunner to today's European Union (EU). Spain developed a close relationship not only with other European states but with the United States as well. After joining the EEC, the Spanish economy prospered, with steady growth in the gross national product (GNP) and a significant decline in unemployment.

The country's political challenges have not been so easily solved, however. Terrorist attacks by the main Basque separatist group, the ETA, continue to plague the country. Although not marked by violence, a similar campaign for regional autonomy persists in Catalonia, and friction continues with the British over the status of Gibraltar. In many ways, though, Spain has come full circle—having lost an empire, Spaniards are busy remaking their country and their destiny. In recent years, hundreds of thousands of immigrants, most of them from Spain's former colonies, have added to the country's economic development and cultural mix. Spain is poised to secure a role as one of Europe's leading economic powers and a powerful player in the new political dynamic of the European Union, as well as on the global stage. As always, there is frequently a price to pay for choosing greater international involvement, as the terrorist attacks in Madrid in March of 2004 attest. In spite of such tragic events, geography and history will ensure that migration, invasion, and trade will likely remain important themes in Spain's future development.

CHAPTER

4

People and Culture

Over the last 3,000 years, a multitude of peoples have entered and settled the Iberian Peninsula, including Greeks, Celts, Germanic tribes, Romans, Arabs, and Berbers. The Spanish people, therefore, share a highly varied ethnic and cultural background. Some regional groups, especially Basques and Catalans, have for centuries preserved a separate identity, rooted in a distinct language and customs. In addition, in recent years, scores of immigrants have added to the diversity of Spain's population. Roman Catholicism, once a cultural element that most Spaniards held in common, has lost ground as a cultural unifier in recent decades. As has always been the case, Spain's people and culture are changing. This chapter discusses the dynamic character of the country's population and culture.

POPULATION

Spain's population shows many characteristics common to economically developed countries, particularly those in Western Europe. The total population of the country in 2006 is estimated at between 40 and 43 million people. If current trends continue, Spain's population will actually reach ZPG (zero population growth) and begin to decline in the near future; however, the fertility rate has fallen well below that of population replacement. Currently, the population is growing at a rate of about 0.15 percent per year, most of the gain resulting from immigration. Were this rate of gain to continue unchanged, it would take an estimated 517 years for the country's population to double! Such figures have little relevance in long-term population dynamics. This is because, historically, population trends in any large group of humans frequently change in a few generations. Today, Spain's population is growing quite slowly, and it is reasonable to expect the pattern to continue in the foreseeable future.

Several factors contribute to Spain's low rate of population growth. Since the 1960s, many social values have changed. For example, the use of contraception among women has dramatically increased, despite opposition from the Roman Catholic Church. Spanish women have entered the workforce in increasing numbers during recent decades. Marriages have declined, and the age of first marriage has increased substantially. Average family size has also declined. All of these trends have led not only to low population growth, but also to a rise in the average age of the Spanish population. These trends are typical of economically advanced countries.

Since World War II, migration has played an important role in Spain's demographics. Poor economic conditions and the repression of the Franco regime caused hundreds of thousands of Spaniards to emigrate between 1950 and 1975. Most went to other European countries, but many moved to South America, with a smaller number leaving for the United States and Canada. The emergence of democracy and economic expansion in the late 1980s slowed this movement, and since the late 1990s, a new trend has developed—the arrival of millions of immigrants on Spain's shores. The majority of these new residents come from North Africa, and many enter the country illegally. Spanish society is becoming more multiethnic, a trait increasingly evident in the country's larger cities, which now feature ethnic neighborhoods and districts.

SETTLEMENT

A country's settlement patterns typically reveal a good deal about economic development, political cohesion, and even social and cultural divisions. The term *settlement* implies an emphasis on distribution—*where* people live often determines *how* they live. Spain's population density—that is, the country's total population, divided by the total area of Spain—stands at about 200 people per square mile (77 per square kilometer). This is a relatively low figure when compared to most West European countries. The population-density figures for an entire country are almost always misleading, however. In Spain, the population of just 4 of the country's 18 regions (Madrid, Catalonia, Valencia, and Andalucía) accounts for almost 50 percent of the entire population!

The Spanish people are highly urbanized, meaning that they mostly live in cities. A full 77 percent of the people fall into this category, a higher percentage than that found in France or Italy, and about the same as that of the United States. The high rate of urbanization is the result of a decades-long shift of the population from poorer, predominantly rural provinces toward the larger urban areas. This trend accelerated in the last two decades of Franco's rule, as economic opportunities vanished in the countryside and jobs were created in Spain's industrial centers. As a result, several provinces in central Spain have some of the lowest population densities in all of Europe.

For example, the provinces of Soria (in Old Castile) and Guadalajara (in New Castile) both have population densities under 10 persons per square mile (4 per square kilometer).

The contrast between Spain's sprawling, cosmopolitan urban centers and the abandoned, sometimes desolate rural districts has been highlighted by the recent wave of immigration from abroad. Immigrants from the developing world almost invariably choose to settle in larger cities, and approximately 10 percent of Madrid's population is made up of foreigners. There seems to be little hope of recovery for many of the poorer rural provinces in Spain. Most young people continue to flee the countryside, drawn by the attractions and opportunities offered by metropolitan areas.

Spain's urban landscape is dominated by its largest city, Madrid, which with slightly more than 3 million people holds about 7 percent of the country's population. Madrid is more than twice as large as the next largest city, Barcelona, the country's most important seaport, which is home to about 1.5 million people. In Spain, only these two cities contain at least a million inhabitants. There are, however, 18 additional cities that have at least 200,000 residents! Two cities of particular importance are Valencia (750,000), in the southeast, and Seville (659,000), in the southwest. Both are regional industrial centers that have grown substantially over the last 20 years, an expansion fueled by Spain's entry into the European Economic Community (later the European Union) in 1986.

ETHNIC GROUPS

Spain's numerous ethnic groups are distinguished primarily by differences in language and geographic region. Ethnicity in Spain is not typically defined by religious differences, except in the case of recent immigrants, especially Muslims. Several ethnic groups in Spain are regionally concentrated and have maintained a strong identity, despite efforts at assimilation by the Castilian-speaking majority.

Madrid, Spain's largest city, is located on the Manzanares River in the center of the country. Founded in the ninth century by the Moors, the city was captured by the Spanish in 1083 and became Spain's capital in 1607. Pictured here is the Metropolis building at the intersection of Calle de Alcalá and Gran Via.

Basques possess a distinctive language (see "Language," later in this chapter) and customs, and their origins remain uncertain. It is clear, however, that they have lived in Iberia for thousands of years. They occupy the northeastern corner of Spain and southwestern France, with about two-thirds of the Basques residing in Spain. Some Basques want to separate from Spain and form an independent state. For several decades, they have pursued a campaign of violence, hoping to achieve this goal (see Chapter 5, "Government and Politics").

The ethnic distinctiveness of the Catalonians, like that of the Basques, is rooted in their language and history. During the nineteenth century, Catalan flowered as a literary language, after several centuries of suppression of Catalonians at the hands of Castilian rulers. At that time, essayists and poets published widely in the Catalan language, reinforcing the separate linguistic identity of the region. Catalonia, like a number of regions of Spain, has a tradition of *fueros*, a collective of traditional laws and customs that were suppressed during the Franco era. In 1978, Catalonian autonomy, based on linguistic differences and fueros, was reestablished as a result of the new constitution. Two years later, a referendum supporting autonomy for Catalonia received more than two-thirds of the popular vote.

A group that has had a profound influence on Spanish culture has been the Gitanos (Gypsies), or as they refer to themselves, the Roma. The Gitanos are concentrated in southern Spain, where their existence was first recorded in 1425. Although believed for centuries to have migrated from Egypt, there is indisputable linguistic evidence that the Roma migrated to Europe from India. For most of their history, they were persecuted in Spain (as they were elsewhere in Europe). Ironically, though, the Gitanos contributed one of the most distinctive elements of Spanish culture—the singing and dancing style known as *flamenco*. Traditionally nomadic, today most Gitanos live in settled communities but continue to suffer social and economic discrimination at the hands of the majority.

LANGUAGE

Many people believe that Spanish is a single language. In reality, however, there are several dialects of the language in Spain alone and dozens throughout the Spanish-speaking world. The dominant variant in Spain today is Castilian Spanish. Castilian was a dialect of Spanish that developed in the principality of Castile, where it emerged as a literary language in the Middle Ages. As the Muslims gradually lost control of the country, Castilian Spanish replaced Arabic in the south and Latin in the north as the dominant language of literature and education across most of the country. In 1714, King Philip V decreed Castilian the official language of Spain and its empire. As the language of the empire, Castilian Spanish was carried across the globe and eventually evolved into various dialects but all mutually intelligible.

Castilian did not completely displace the regional languages of Spain, however. Some regions retain a strong sense of identity based primarily on their languages. In some instances, these tongues are recognized as official languages, along with Castilian. A good example is the Catalan language, or, as its speakers call it, Catala. Catalan is a Romance tongue spoken by about 6 million people in eastern Spain, some parts of southern France, and the Balearic Islands. The use of Catalan nearly died out after Castilian was declared Spain's official language, but the language was revived in the late 1800s. Today, it is the main component of Catalonian identity.

In the far northwest corner of Spain, adjacent to Portugal, lies the province of Galicia. Here Galego (often referred to as Galician) is a widely spoken language. In fact, a higher percentage of people in Galicia speak Galego than speak Catalan in Catalonia, or the Basque language in northeastern Spain. Galego is more closely related to Portuguese than to Castilian, and like Catalan, it serves as an official language for its region.

The Basque people of northeastern Spain speak a unique language, which they call Euskara, and others simply call Basque. Euskara is not related to any of the languages in Europe, or for that matter in the entire world, and linguistic geographers are unable to trace its origins. It is a highly complex tongue, with numerous dialects and subdialects, and outsiders typically struggle to master just the basics of the language. Individual villages in the Basque region frequently have their own dialect of the language. It was not until 1968 that a standardized, literary form of Euskara was created by the Basque linguist Luis Mitxelena.

RELIGION

Religion has played a vital role in Spain's history. This is clearly evident from the multitude of religious structures found in all regions of the country. Most of them are centuries old, but some are quite modern. These range from the spectacular Alhambra, an Islamic palace, in Granada, to the unique modernist El Temple Expiatori de la Sagrada Familia, in Barcelona. The latter, begun in 1883 by Antoni Gaudí, is probably the most unusual Roman Catholic cathedral in the world. In contrast, the cathedral at Compostela in northern Spain is almost 1,000 years old. Many rituals and festivals observed by Spaniards are historically rooted in its religions.

Most Spaniards remain nominally Roman Catholic, with some surveys showing that between 80 and 94 percent of the population claim to follow the faith. Roman Catholicism was the official religion of Spain from 1851 to 1978. In 1978, however, a new constitution limited the political role of the Church in Spanish affairs and allowed citizens more religious freedom. During recent decades, the Spanish have become increasingly secularized. Many young people have abandoned the religious habits of the generations before them, including regular attendance at Mass. In general, many in Spanish society no longer follow the Church's teachings on contraception, abortion, or homosexuality, a sign of the weakening influence of the Church on Spanish society. The changing fortunes of the Church may also be seen in the declining numbers of young people who enter the service of the Church, either as priests or nuns.

However, some faiths are growing in the country; although the total number of followers in each case remains relatively small. Some Protestant denominations, particularly Evangelicals, Mormons, and Jehovah's Witnesses, appear to be gaining in numbers. Even so, Protestants continue to represent less than 10 percent of the population. Unlike the Roman Catholic Church, Protestant churches in Spain do not receive support

Despite the fact that 80 to 94 percent of Spain's population consider themselves Roman Catholic, recent surveys indicate that only about 18 percent attend Mass regularly. The young penitents pictured here during a Holy Week procession in Segura do not reflect the growing trend toward secularism in Spain, especially among the youth.

from the government. As would be expected, the growth of Protestantism is of great concern to Catholic leaders both in Spain and in the Vatican.

During the Middle Ages, the Spanish Inquisition eliminated most of the Muslim and Jewish communities in the country. By the late twentieth century, however, both groups were reemerging in Spain. In recent years, significant numbers of Muslims have immigrated into the country, particularly from North Africa. The Spanish enclaves of Ceuta and Melilla, on Morocco's northern coast, hold a majority of Islamic believers. In total, Muslims account for about 3 percent of religious believers in Spain. Muslims in Spain tend to be devout, and in general, religion plays a larger role in their lives than is the case with their Christian counterparts. The religious landscape of Spain has fundamentally changed in the last generation. In the future, it certainly will continue to be modified by migration, the opposing forces of conversion and secularization, and other forces in Spanish society.

SPAIN'S DEMOGRAPHIC AND CULTURAL FUTURE

Spain's cultural and demographic landscape is rapidly changing. The social and economic shifts in Spanish society over the last generation have, in turn, led to new challenges. The country's low rate of population growth means that immigration is the only means of increasing the labor supply. This reality will inevitably modify the nature of what it means to be Spanish. Similarly, the aging Spanish population brings with it social and economic challenges that must be addressed if the country is to prosper. Perhaps most important, the country must strike a balance between a strong, unitary identity and regional ethnicities, particularly in the Basque country and Catalonia. How the Spanish people meet these new prospects and challenges will determine the character and success of the country in the new millennium.

CHAPTER

5

Government and Politics

THE TRANSITION TO DEMOCRACY

From 1939 to 1975, Spain was ruled by a dictator, General Francisco Franco. With Franco's death in 1975, Spain moved rapidly, under the leadership of King Juan Carlos and his prime minister, Adolfo Suarez, to create a democratic system and build a civil society. In 1977, the *Cortes*, the Spanish legislature, approved a proposal to create a parliament with two legislatures and to legalize opposition political parties. The next year, a new constitution was approved. It established a parliamentary monarchy, eliminated Roman Catholicism as the official religion, and granted significant autonomy to the country's regions.

Essentially, the new constitution dismantled the strong centralized state of the Franco era. The following three decades have witnessed the development of a strong democratic tradition in Spanish politics, a trend the Spanish public seems to favor overwhelmingly.

King Juan Carlos, pictured here standing below Spain's coat of arms during a meeting of the Spanish Parliament, was named ruler of Spain shortly after the death of Francisco Franco in 1975. Under Juan Carlos, Spain has become a democratic constitutional monarchy and has promoted free elections.

THE EXECUTIVE BRANCH

Spain's form of government is a parliamentary monarchy. The king is the head of state, whereas the government is headed by a prime minister. The prime minister is technically appointed by the king, but he or she must first be elected to the post by the Congress of Deputies, one of the branches of the legislature. The political party that holds the most seats in the Congress of Deputies typically is able to place its candidate in the position of prime minister. Occasionally, it becomes necessary for a party to form alliances with other parties holding seats in the Congress, in order to elect a leader. The prime minister is responsible for foreign policy and many aspects of domestic policy. He or she (to date, those holding the position have been male) formulates policy with the assistance of a cabinet, the members of which he or she nominates and who are invested by the king. King Juan Carlos has been the Spanish sovereign since 1975, when the monarchy was restored in the wake of Franco's death. The prime minister also has the power to dissolve the Spanish parliament and call for early elections to the legislative branch, if he so chooses.

The current prime minister is José Luis Rodríguez Zapatero, who heads the leftist Spanish Socialist Workers Party (PSOE). The PSOE victory in the elections of March 2004 was unexpected. Many observers believe that the terrorist bombings that occurred only three days before the general election were the primary reason José Maria Anzar was defeated. Prior to the tragedy, his center-right People's Party appeared to be headed for reelection. Anzar had nurtured a close relationship with the United States. He had even sent Spanish forces to Iraq in 2003 to support the U.S. effort to oust Saddam Hussein. Many Spaniards felt that the Madrid bombings were in retaliation for Spain's role in Iraq. Immediately after he was elected, Zapatero ordered the withdrawal of Spanish troops from the Middle East.

LEGISLATIVE AND JUDICIAL BRANCHES OF GOVERNMENT

The legislative branch of the Spanish government is known as the Cortes Generales (often simply referred to as the Cortes) and consists of two bodies: the Congress of Deputies and the Senate. The Congress of Deputies is larger, and members elected to this body typically serve for a term of four years, although the term may be shorter, if the prime minister calls for early elections. Representatives in the Congress are directly elected from the country's 50 provinces and the autonomous cities of Ceuta and Melilla. The number of deputies from each province is determined in a system of proportional representation based on population. In other words, those provinces with a greater population are granted a larger number of representatives, a system similar to that used for the U.S. House of Representatives. In total, there are 350 deputies in the Congress.

In addition, the Congress of Deputies holds certain powers over the prime minister. The Congress must approve the prime minister by vote before he or she takes the oath of office before the king. In addition, Congress may bring charges of treason or other crimes against the prime minister and members of his cabinet. If the Congress approves a motion of censure against a sitting prime minister, the prime minister must resign the post. The process is similar to impeachment in the U.S. system of government.

The second chamber of the parliament is the Senate. Each of Spain's provinces elects four senators, and the Balearic and Canary Islands also elect senators. Moreover, each of the country's autonomous provinces elects a single senator. Those with a population of at least one million inhabitants are represented by an additional senator for every million residents. This brings the total number of members of the Senate to 254, a body more than twice the size of the U.S. Senate. The Senate has the authority to veto or change any laws that are passed by the Congress. In reality, however, the Senate is not as powerful as the Congress of Deputies, since that body may override a Senate veto with a simple majority vote of its membership.

Spain's judicial system is controlled by the General Council of the Judiciary, a body that appoints judges to the country's courts. There are 20 members of the General Council, with half being chosen by the Congress of Deputies and half by the Senate. The highest court is the Supreme Court, which functions much like the U.S. Supreme Court, except that it does not decide constitutional questions. Issues of constitutionality are resolved by the Constitutional Court, a body of 12 judges who serve nine-year terms. The legislative branch appoints eight of the members, the executive two, and the General Council appoints the remaining two judges to the Court. The court rules on the constitutionality of laws at both the federal and regional levels and can also determine the legality of international treaties into which Spain has entered.

LOCAL AUTONOMY

The 1978 constitution created a federal system in which much political control was decentralized. Much of the authority was shifted from the national administration in Madrid to Spain's numerous regions. Between 1978 and 1983, however, the country experienced a political crisis. Various regions demanded greater control over policy, and some, such as the Basque provinces and Catalonia, appeared ready to declare independence. Regionalism, long suppressed under Franco, threatened the integrity of the country and the national administration's ability to govern.

The Law on the Harmonization of the Autonomy Process, passed in 1981, resolved many of the issues surrounding regionalization. At the same time, it restructured Spain's fundamental political geography. The country was divided into 17 autonomous regions, including 3 regions outside the Iberian mainland (the Balearic Islands, the Canary Islands, and Ceuta and Melilla). Most regions were further subdivided into provinces. Catalonia, the Basque country, Galicia, and other regions where languages other than Castilian Spanish are used typically elevated those tongues to an official status equal to that of Castilian.

Each autonomous region has its own government structures, generally outlined in a statute of autonomy. Each region has a designated capital city, and regions adopt a regional flag, which is usually flown alongside the Spanish national flag. The regional government is headed by a president, who is elected by the regional legislature. There is a regional court system, as well, but decisions of regional courts are subject to review by federal courts, including the Supreme Court. Regional governments are generally responsible for implementing policy on local economic development, managing resources, maintaining social welfare and health-care systems, and supporting cultural and recreational activities. The regional legislatures also have the authority to levy and collect taxes, which they use as sources of revenue in addition to federal funds provided to the regions from the central government in Madrid.

TERRORISM AND POLITICAL TURMOIL

On March 11, 2004, a series of explosions ripped through several commuter trains in Madrid, killing 192 people and wounding more than 1,000. The bombs were the work of Islamic militants believed to be linked to al-Qaeda and Osama bin Laden. This barbarous attack was one of the worst acts of terrorism to effect Spain. Unfortunately, it certainly was not a unique experience for the country. Spain has been battling domestic terrorism since the 1960s, when a radical Basque group, the Euskadi Ta Askatasuna (ETA), initiated a violent campaign in an effort to win independence for the Basque region.

The ETA was formed in 1959, with the goal of eventually establishing a separate Basque state. Since its founding, the ETA has been responsible for hundreds of bombings and assassinations of Spanish officials. In 1973, it murdered Luis Blanco, a high-ranking member of the Franco regime. And in the 1990s, ETA was implicated in plots to kill both José Anzar, the country's future prime minister, and King Juan Carlos.

The group also targets Basque businessmen who fail to pay extortion money that ETA utilizes to conduct its activities.

According to some political observers, ETA's numbers are small, they are poorly educated, and most members are over 40 years of age. The organization does not appear to have connections to al-Qaeda or other Islamic groups but in the past has formed alliances with the Irish Republican Army and possibly other radicals.

Since 2000, ETA has curtailed its activities to some degree. It continues to target police, government officials, and innocent civilians, however, as was the case with a car bomb in central Madrid that injured dozens in October 2001. In an effort to undermine support for ETA, Spain's Supreme Court ruled in 2003 that ETA's political branch, Batasuna, was an illegal organization. In total, nearly 800 people have died and hundreds more have been injured and maimed as a result of violence by ETA since it was established.

Despite the continued activities of ETA, and more recently a rise in the activities of Islamic militants on Spanish soil, the stability of the Spanish state and Spanish democracy appears sound. Civil liberties and the rule of law, two pillars of democracy long ignored under Franco, have become an essential part of the foundation of Spanish society. A telling sign of the country's commitment to both is indicated by the government's willingness to prosecute members of the security forces who abuse their authority. Such action would have been unthinkable under the Franco dictatorship.

FOREIGN RELATIONS AND TERRITORIAL DISPUTES

The three decades of Franco rule were difficult years for Spain in the international community. Many governments, especially in Europe, imposed sanctions on the Spanish regime. These actions were taken in the hope that such pressures would force Franco to reduce human rights abuses and allow more political freedom. This strategy had a limited effect

The Basque people of northern Spain have long fought for their independence from the Spanish. Several groups make up the Basque National Liberation Movement, including Batasuna, members of whom are pictured here marching at a rally in Bilbao, Spain. The rally was to support peace negotiations between the Spanish government and Batasuna, in hopes of ending the three-decade-long conflict.

on Spanish domestic politics, although it did succeed in isolating the country to a considerable degree in its international relations. With Franco's death in 1975, Spain's relationship with its neighbors changed dramatically. By 1986, the European Economic Community (EEC) rewarded Spain for making reforms in its government by granting the country membership. This, together with Spain's long-delayed entry into NATO (North Atlantic Treaty Organization) in 1982, represented a key step in the process of integrating Spain back into the international community.

When Spain joined the European Economic Community (which became the European Union, or EU) in 1994, the country experienced several political and economic changes. Like all members of the EU, the Spanish government has made the decision to sacrifice a certain amount of sovereignty in order to secure the benefits of membership. Residents of some European countries have indicated reservations toward membership in the organization, but Spaniards appear to support their country's role in the EU. On February 20, 2005, Spanish voters strongly supported the EU Constitution in a national referendum, with nearly 77 percent of the vote cast in favor of the document. This was in stark contrast to the referendums held in France and the Netherlands, both charter members of the European Economic Community, just three months later. Both the French and the Dutch rejected the constitution, sending shock waves through the capitals of Europe. Ironically, the Spanish, long Europe's outsiders, appear to be one of the continent's staunchest supporters of European integration.

Unfortunately, the reintegration of the country into the European community did not lead to the resolution of several long-standing territorial disputes with neighboring countries. The most serious disagreement concerns the status of Gibraltar, a British enclave located on Spain's southern coast. The "Rock," as it is sometimes called, is quite small—its total area is less than three square miles (eight square kilometers)—and has little economic importance aside from tourist revenues. Gibraltar, however, commands the northern side of the Strait of Gibraltar, the water passage between the Atlantic Ocean and the Mediterranean Sea. Political geographers refer to such a strategic position that controls access between two bodies of water as a "choke point." Spain lost Gibraltar to the British in 1704 as a result of the War of Spanish Succession, and the territory has remained under British control ever since. The Spanish government periodically demands the return of Gibraltar, but this seems unlikely in the foreseeable future. The results of a referendum in 2002 indicated that 99 percent of Gibraltar's residents do not favor Spanish rule.

Indeed, Spain has similar territorial issues with Morocco over the Spanish enclaves of Ceuta and Melilla, on the northern coast of that country. Ceuta controls the southern side of the Strait of Gibraltar, whereas Melilla is located on a peninsula about 100 miles to the east. Spain acquired Melilla in 1497, and Ceuta was obtained from Portugal in 1580, when the Portuguese and Spanish crowns were briefly joined. Both territories were granted provincial status according to the 1978 constitution, and both elect representatives to the Spanish Parliament. Most residents of both enclaves are Muslims, and many do not speak Spanish as their first language. Despite their incorporation into Spain's political system, Morocco continues to claim sovereignty over both areas, and this represents a simmering source of tension between the two neighbors.

After being considered an outsider for much of the twentieth century, Spain has regained a place at the forefront of European and world affairs. As European integration continues apace, the country is poised to assume a leading role in that process. Leadership on the regional and world stages brings with it greater influence. However, integration also brings greater responsibilities and risks—a lesson the Spanish people learned tragically on March 11, 2004. Spain has not yet satisfactorily met all of its domestic challenges. The ETA remains a threat to stability, and strong regional forces continue to undermine the legitimacy and future of the state. When viewed against the backdrop of the repression and isolation of the Franco years, though, the Spanish people have achieved tremendous progress. This trend seems likely to hold its course well into the twenty-first century.

6

Spain's Economy

In recent years, the European Union economic zone has struggled. Almost all developed countries throughout the world, including the United States, have suffered from an economic slowdown and irritating stagnation. During that same period, however, Spain's economy continued to grow. In fact, its economic output expanded twice as fast as that of the European Union. This amazing progress has been the direct result of a successful economic transformation that began several decades ago.

Today, the Spanish economy is changing in many ways. Of greatest importance, perhaps, is that Spaniards are readily accepting a change in attitude; that is, they now understand how the economic world works and are eager to become a part of the global economic community. First and foremost, the old fascistic idea that self-sufficiency was to be the national economic (and political) goal has been replaced. The Spanish Kingdom, Franco decided in his early days, was to have an economic system that wasn't dependent on the outside world. Such views of economic self-sufficiency are commonplace with various totalitarian regimes throughout the world. If a government can control a country's economy, it can easily control many other aspects of the country and its people. This was Franco's goal, although history has shown that it was painfully counterproductive.

By the 1960s, it was becoming apparent that Spain had to find another economic direction. The route chosen was to open its economic boundaries. This proved to be the right move, because since open trade was implemented, Spain's economy has shown continued growth. At first, progress was significant but still viewed as something unexpected, strange, or even undeserved. When people have been oppressed for a period of time, it can take some time for them to realize the benefits of change. Since 1975, when the demise of the Franco regime ended a sad chapter in the country's political history, Spain embraced democracy and a fully free economy.

SPAIN IN THE EUROPEAN UNION

Becoming a member of the European Union in 1986 proved to be a good economic decision for Spain. Membership opened borders to an ever-growing common market and millions of potential customers for Spanish companies willing to expand outside the national boundaries. Since the 1980s, two major economic concerns have been resolved: Unemployment has been drastically reduced, and inflation controlled. Unemployment rates that once soared to more than 20 percent have been halved to around 10 percent in two decades.

Conservative fiscal policy contributed to lowering the annual inflation rate to 2 to 3 percent, a range comparable to that of other developed countries. In 1999, Spain made another vital economic decision: It adopted the EU's *euro* as its currency. With the European Union's expansion eastward, prospects for Spain are bright, especially for its tertiary (service) sector.

Spain joined the European Union (EU) in 1986, and adopted its currency, the euro, in 1999. However, the euro did not officially become legal tender until January 1, 2002, when 12 countries began using it. Pictured here is a fruit-stall worker selling oranges in Valencia, Spain, shortly before the euro became legal tender. The price of the oranges is listed in both pesetas (the former currency) and euros.

One negative economic aspect, often shared with other EU members, is a rather high amount of public debt. This presents a difficult obstacle and significant burden for an emerging economy, because higher debt means less money is available to direct into public and other projects.

Another serious issue for Spain is the matter of production reciprocity—the amount of agricultural products each member state is allowed to produce. In order to prevent over-production and provide equal rights for each of its members, the European Union's bodies keep strict control on agricultural production quotas. Therefore, if a particular country's farmers plant more acreage or produce more crops than their quota, they face penalties. Fines can be levied and produce destroyed. Livestock raising and fishing face similar quotas. To some countries, this might not appear to be an important economic issue, but to Spain, a major producer of agricultural products and harvester of marine resources, such sanctions can be painful. The country's agricultural exports amount to some $25 to $30 billion annually, accounting for about 3 percent of the gross domestic product (GDP).

AGRICULTURE

Agriculture remains an important contributor to the economy of many countries, including Spain. Today, you can visit a supermarket and find many agricultural products from the Mediterranean realm, most of which will undoubtedly be of Spanish origin. These products will include olives and olive oil, grapes, wine, citrus and other fruits, a wide variety of vegetables, various types of grain, and more.

Spain is the world's largest producer of olive oil and ranks third in the production of wine (with production nearly twice that of the United States). Agriculture is dependent on conditions of the natural environment. As you learned in Chapter 2, the climate of Spain is quite dry and the country experiences severe drought during the summer growing season. If it were not for the achievements of modern technology, Spanish agriculture would be less productive. Most crops depend on irrigation; sprinkling and soaking systems are dispersed throughout the country's agricultural areas to compensate for the lack of precipitation.

Although much of the agricultural land could still be productive with little or no irrigation, crops would suffer from lack of water. Without irrigation, the yields of most crops would be very low, hardly justifying the expense of planting, tilling, and harvesting. A similar situation exists in California, where most farmers could not stay in business were it not for irrigation. In 2005, agriculture in Spain experienced a huge setback, as the country suffered one of the worst droughts in the last half century.

Meat production is an extremely important contributor to Spain's agricultural economy. Both domestic and international demand has soared in recent decades. Many producers are now shifting from crop farming to more profitable and less environmentally demanding cattle raising. The fishing industry, as well, is trying to survive restrictive quotas and to continue to prosper. Spaniards rank among the world's top per-capita consumers of seafood, which is a vital and very healthy component of the Mediterranean diet. Spain's national dish, *paella,* includes a variety of marine delicacies, including shrimp, squid, clams, and mussels.

INDUSTRY AND SERVICE

Although agriculture is the most visible economic activity on the Spanish landscape, its contribution to the country's economy is relatively insignificant. Secondary (manufacturing) and tertiary (services) industries together account for about 97 percent of the country's total productivity. This is not an anomaly; rather, it is commonplace among mature and emerging economies. Unless something extraordinary happens, such as warfare, national economies generally pass through similar stages. Initially, a less developed country (LDC) is involved in primary economic activities—those based on the exploitation of natural resources. Such industries include agriculture, fishing, mining, and logging. Most laborers are engaged in these activities, which require hard work but little formal education. Wages are low.

In the second stage, manufacturing industries appear. Because of the need for factory workers, industrial cities such as Madrid grow rapidly. Wages are generally higher, and laborers must possess some knowledge and skills. Before the enlargement of the European Union, including eastward expansion, Spain benefited from having lower labor costs than the rest of Western Europe. In order to cut expenses, many companies moved production plants to Spain, which helped fuel the country's industrial expansion. Ford Motor Company has been assembling vehicles in Spain for its overseas distribution network since 1976. The German automaker Volkswagen invested heavily in the Spanish automobile manufacturer SEAT as soon as Spain joined the European Union in 1986. The joint venture proved highly successful and at the same time rapidly revitalized a sluggish Spanish automobile industry. Foreign investments have also been responsible for steady growth in many other industries, the most important of which is the production of chemicals and pharmaceuticals.

As people move from the country into the cities, a cash economy based on the sale and purchase of needed goods replaces bartering and trading. At least some formal education is needed if a person is to successfully adapt to urban living. As urban populations grow, a host of services are required to meet the needs of the people. Goods and people must be transported; sanitation and health care must be maintained; education must be provided from primary grades through college and university, including technical and vocational training; police and fire protection must be provided, as must a variety of public utilities. These are just some of the services that employed nearly 70 percent of the Spanish labor force in 2006.

In this third stage, agriculture and manufacturing begin to decline in importance. People need and demand services and are willing to pay for them. Many service industries require a well-educated and highly skilled workforce, resulting in much better paid workers. Most services are supported by a highly developed technological network. Examples include international banking, stock exchanges, or the airline

Shortly after Spain joined the European Union in 1986, German automobile manufacturer Volkswagen began investing heavily in Spanish automobile manufacturer SEAT (Spanish Corporation of Private Cars). Pictured here is an automobile lot at SEAT's manufacturing plant in Martorell, Spain. The plant annually produces 450,000 cars and SEAT has distribution centers in 50 countries.

industry. Nowadays, in developed countries, even agriculture can become more of a service industry, rather than simply a means for providing food for a family. Huge corporations may own land and hire workers that, in turn, earn money for corporate executives and stockholders, who have never seen the fields from which their income is derived.

Today, tourism has become Spain's most important service industry. It is a multibillion-dollar business. With more than 50 million visitors each year, Spain ranks second among the world's countries (behind France and just ahead of the United States) in its number of international visitors. In addition to its direct economic impact, tourism stimulates development in other sectors of the economy, such as retail sales and real estate. Profits generated from tourism can give a huge boost to a country's GDP. Spain has greatly benefited from its scenic mountain and coastal landscapes, its rich culture and history, and its able workforce.

ENERGY

Unfortunately, not all news relating to Spain's economy is good. As a country's economy expands, so, too, does its need for energy. Little energy is consumed by people engaged in primary economic activities. As manufacturing increases, cities and urban populations grow. As a result, the need for transportation and other services expand, and more energy is needed and consumed. Simply stated, economically developed countries use (and waste) much more energy than do LDCs. A few paragraphs earlier, for example, we discussed two important developments in the Spanish automobile industry. Today, Spaniards enjoy the benefits of hard work and the country's progress. They own millions of automobiles and drive billions of miles each year, which, of course, has vastly expanded their dependence on petroleum.

Spain's energy requirements are much greater than the country's domestic supplies. In fact, about three-quarters of all energy consumed must be imported. Oil and natural gas are vital to Spain's further economic expansion and the standard of living enjoyed by its people. Obtaining these energy resources, however, poses a sensitive geopolitical dilemma. A vast majority of the country's oil and gas imports come from North Africa and the Middle East. This situation (which many countries face, including the United States) leaves Spain vulnerable to global geopolitical events. In response to this vulnerability, Spain is taking steps to eliminate dependency on foreign energy supplies and to generate its own energy wherever possible. In fact, in 2005, it ranked first among the world's nations in energy production from alternative sources such as wind and the sun.

Wind farming is one area in which excellent progress has been made. During the coming decade, Spain hopes to develop its wind-generating capacity to 40 percent of all electricity produced. This plan may seem ambitious, but by 2006, Spain already ranked second among the world's countries in harnessing wind power. Much of Europe's electricity is produced by nuclear plants. In the aftermath of the Chernobyl incident, however, public support for this energy source has declined sharply. It seems likely that within the next decade or two, all of Spain's nine existing nuclear plants will be shut down.

INFRASTRUCTURE

Infrastructure refers to a country's systems of transportation, communication, and other systems that move people, materials, information, and other items. Both current and previous governments realized the importance of a well-developed network of roads, railroads, airports, and telecommunications. Without these linkages, the country surely would fall behind other developed nations. Today, Spain is investing huge resources in upgrading its existing networks and building new facilities. Some of the projects are private, others are government supported, and still others involve joint ventures with foreign investors. The most ambitious construction project currently under consideration is the erection of a bridge to connect Europe and Africa at the Strait of Gibraltar. If completed, the 9-mile (14.5-kilometer) bridge would be the only direct nonwater link between Europe and Africa.

The railroad network is undergoing change, and more advanced high-speed trains are replacing the older tracks and technology. Learning a valuable lesson from their northern neighbor, France, Spanish planners, engineers, and politicians finally came to realize that their fellow citizens can enjoy the benefits of high-speed railways. In terms of speed, cost, and ease of travel, French "bullet trains" are able to successfully compete with air carriers for passengers. Spanish authorities hope to achieve similar results. A fast and reliable railroad network, it is believed, will offer relief from the country's overcrowded highways.

In the field of telecommunications, Spain has not kept pace with developments in most other Western European countries. However, considerable improvements have been made in basic communications, such as cellular phone networks. Most of the country is covered with cell-phone facilities provided by several competing companies. Today, there are twice as many mobile phones in Spain than there are home phones. The number of Internet users is rapidly growing, and even in the remote countryside, the Internet has become a part of everyday life. Compared to the best developed EU countries, however, growth of latest technology telecommunications has been slow. Corporations and other businesses simply have not had the capital to invest in this area of development. As the economy grows and more capital becomes available, this situation will change.

TRADE

Direct foreign investments in the Spanish economy are steadily growing and becoming more diversified. This is good news, because diversification means that investments are long-term, rather than short-term opportunities. As expected, the largest investors are from the European Union and North America. Even though two-thirds of Spain's foreign trade is conducted with other EU members, in recent years, Spain's relationship with the United States has improved. In 2005, Spain exported more than $5 billion worth of products to the United States. This figure is rather small when compared to the country's $175 billion of total exports (2005), but it is rising each year. Spanish companies are aware of the many possibilities offered by the U.S. market. This is especially true considering the rise in the Spanish-speaking population in the United States. Latin America, a region with which Spain has close historical and cultural ties, is the country's third-largest regional trading partner. About half of Spain's exports are finished products that contribute the added value of human labor and application of technology.

Spain's import partners are basically the same as those to whom it exports products. Trade with countries of Western and central Europe is strongly favored by the European Union. With a common currency, the euro, prices are regulated and nothing is lost in currency exchange between countries. Because of rising demands among Spanish consumers and an expanding economy (particularly the need for petroleum and other raw materials), imports are greater than exports, creating a negative trade balance.

In order to balance its budget, the government must provide additional revenue from elsewhere, or go into debt by borrowing money from international creditors. Every time a country has a negative trade balance—that is, it imports more than exports—it faces critical economic problems. Spain's goal is to further diversify and increase its exports, while reducing dependence on imported energy.

7

Regions of Spain

L ike all large countries, the geography of Spain is best studied by visiting its diverse regions and exploring its characteristics. Regions can be identified by their physical features, cultural distinctions, political boundaries, economic functions, or other characteristics. The geographer's goal in dividing any larger region into smaller units is to simplify it. In doing so, though, he or she also emphasizes the generous diversity any large landscape typically offers. This discussion of Spain's regional geography focuses primarily on the largest nine regions of what is known as "Peninsular Spain," or mainland Spain. In addition, mention is made of "offshore Spain"—the Canary and Balearic islands, and the enclaves of Ceuta and Melilla. The population figures provided for various cities typically represent the number of people in the general metropolitan area and are based on recent Spanish government census figures.

ANDALUCÍA

Beginning in the south of Spain, Andalucía is the country's most populous region and the second largest in area. Seven and a half million people live in this part of Spain, or one in every five Spaniards. Andalucía contain's Spain's oldest cities and its most spectacular architecture from the Muslim period. The capital and most populous city is Seville, which now boasts a greater metropolitan area of more than 1,500,000 people. Seville is famous for bullfighting and flamenco music. It was also the home of the legendary Don Juan. Although located approximately 50 miles from the coast, Seville historically served as an important port, until the Guadalquivir River became unnavigable. A mausoleum in the city claims to hold the remains of Christopher Columbus. Seville sits at the heart of one of Spain's most important agricultural regions, and much of the city's industry is devoted to the processing of cotton, wheat, olives, grapes, and other products grown in the surrounding provinces. Granada (450,000) and Cordoba (321,000) were Muslim strongholds when Andalucía was part of the Islamic world, and Granada's Alhambra palace draws tens of thousands of tourists to the city annually. Cordoba served as the capital of the Spanish caliphate and in the early Middle Ages was Europe's most populous city. Other important cities in Andalucía include Almeria (176,000), Malaga (814,000), Cadiz (629,054), and Huelva (141,000), all of which are ports.

NEW CASTILE (CASTILE LA MANCHA)

New Castile is Spain's third-largest region in area but contains fewer than 2 million inhabitants. It includes one of the most famous provinces in the country, La Mancha, immortalized by Miguel de Cervantes in his classic satirical novel, *Don Quixote*. The capital of the region is Toledo (75,000), a Roman settlement that later served as the Visigoth capital, as well as the capital of the old province of Castile

Pictured here is the town of Granada, in the Andalucía region of southern Spain. From 1232 to 1492, Granada was the seat of the Nasrid dynasty, the last Muslim dynasty in Spain.

for several centuries. Toledo was once the center for the production of "Spanish steel," high-quality swords and knives favored by warriors across Europe. Today, the city still produces excellent cutlery. The city was also the home of one of Spain's most famous artists, El Greco, whose works may be found in many of the city's churches and museums. Ciudad Real (65,000) and Guadalajara (66,000) are both historic cities from which many residents commute to Spain's largest city, Madrid.

MADRID

Spain's smallest region is also the location of the country's most populous urban area and national capital, Madrid. The population of greater metropolitan Madrid is approaching 5.5 million residents (3 million within the city), a million more inhabitants than Spain's second-largest city, Barcelona. Approximately 10 percent of the city's residents are recent immigrants, mostly from Latin America and North Africa. King Philip II declared Madrid the capital of the Spanish empire in 1561, but at that time the location was occupied by a relatively small town. With the wealth gained from Spain's far-flung empire, Philip and his successors built the new capital to rival Europe's greatest cities. His task was made easier by the city's location along trade routes running through central Spain. The city was heavily damaged and endured an extended siege during the Spanish Civil War, falling to Franco's forces only in the last year of the conflict. Modern Madrid is the centerpiece of Spain's economy, serving as the location of the nation's major financial markets, its telecommunications, and its banking and insurance industries. In addition, both light and heavy industries have established themselves in the capital, including clothing manufacturing, food processing, and automobile assembly plants. Perhaps one of the most obvious signs of Madrid's worldliness and modernity is the presence of the Warner Brothers Movie World Spain. This American theme park located just south of the city attracts thousands of visitors from Spain and around the world.

OLD CASTILE (CASTILE AND LEON)

Old Castile represents the very heart of Spain, both geographically and philosophically. The region has the largest area in the country, consisting of much of the northern part of the Meseta Central, a large, rugged plateau occupying the middle section of Spain. The regional capital is the old university city of Valladolid (400,000), now a major industrial center and the location of several universities. Valladolid has played a vital role in Spanish history— it is the city where Tomás de Torquemada, the head of the Spanish Inquisition, was born. It is also the city where Christopher Columbus died. The ancient city of Salamanca (156,000) lies in the southwestern corner of the region. Sometimes referred to as La Ciudad Dorada, or the "Golden City," because of the yellowish sandstone used for many of its older buildings, Salamanca is home to Spain's first Christian university. Founded in 1218, the University of Salamanca still draws thousands of students from around the world. Salamanca's rival for beauty may be Segovia (55,000), another historic city located in southern Old Castile. Segovia features a magnificent 2,000-year-old Roman aqueduct that still carries water. It also has a picturesque *alcazar*, or castle, where King Ferdinand and Queen Isabella were married in 1469, thus setting the stage for the Age of Discovery and the establishment of the Spanish empire. The city was declared a World Heritage Site by UNESCO in 1985.

EXTREMADURA

Spain's "wild west," Extremadura is the poorest and most rural region in Peninsular Spain. For decades, many people, especially the young, have been leaving this area for the country's larger cities, which offer better economic and social opportunities. The region's main economic activities are the production of olives and wool; it is a leader in both commodities, as well as cotton and wheat production. However, only a small percentage of visitors to Spain ever venture into this remote corner of the country. Several small but interesting cities and villages dot this rolling landscape. The capital of the region is Merida, a modest settlement of about 50,000 people, and like its neighbor Cáceres (80,000), it was an ancient Roman outpost. The ruins of numerous Roman buildings, including a spectacular theater that is still used to stage Greek and Roman plays, have been excavated at Merida. The most populous city in Extremadura is Badajoz, with 136,000 inhabitants. Situated close to the border with Portugal, Badajoz is a former fortress city that today benefits from trade between the two Iberian members of the EU.

GALICIA

Tucked into the extreme northwest corner of Iberia, Galicia is a unique part of Spain for several reasons. The climate of most of Spain is dry and generally warm, particularly the Meseta Central and Andalucía. Galicia is rainy and cooler, however, and until the late Middle Ages supported forests. The Galicians speak a unique Romance language, Galego, which is more closely related to Portuguese than to Castilian Spanish. Because of the area's cultural distinctiveness, support for autonomy—if not outright independence—has been strongly supported in Galicia for at least a century. Ironically, Galicia is home to the most important Christian shrine in Spain, Santiago de Compostela. During the Middle Ages, Christian pilgrims from every corner of Europe journeyed to the cathedral in this city, believing that it held the bones of Saint James the Apostle. Today, thousands of tourists, some of them on a religious quest and others merely sightseeing, continue this centuries-old tradition.

Galicia's jagged, spectacular coastline attracts many visitors. The shore is broken by numerous narrow, steep bays called *rias*, which resemble the fjords of Norway and Alaska. These indentations offer some shelter from the strong storms that occasionally blow in from the northern Atlantic Ocean. The remote northwestern section of the region's coast is called the *Costa da Morte* (in Galego), or "Coast of Death," so named for the heavy seas and dangerous weather that sometimes plague the area's mariners. The largest port on the western coast is Vigo (420,000), the home of a massive fishing fleet. Galician cuisine is noteworthy for its emphasis on seafood, including dishes prepared from octopus, squid, and a variety of shellfish. At the northern end of the Costa da Morte is the historic city of Corunna (388,000), founded by the Romans and featuring a functioning lighthouse built by Roman engineers. Corunna's sister city, Ferrol (210,000), is the industrial center of Galicia, possessing a large shipyard and steel works. Ferrol also has the distinction of being the birthplace of Francisco Franco, Spain's longtime dictator.

THE BASQUE REGION

The Basque region consists of three provinces abutting France along Spain's northeastern frontier. The provinces are (using the Basque names) Araba, Bizkaia, and Gipuzkoa. The Basques are ethnically distinct, having their own unique language and cultural traditions. Approximately two-thirds of the Basques live in Spain, with the remaining third residing across the border in France. The largest city in the Basque region is Bilbao, the capital of the province of Bizkaia. Greater metropolitan Bilbao is home to almost a million people, and the city has long been a major industrial center and port. About 15 miles (24 kilometers) to the east of Bilbao lies Guernica, a city infamously bombed by a German squadron during the civil war, resulting in thousands of deaths. Guernica is also the site where for centuries Basque leaders have met to direct the affairs of their people and thus has great symbolic importance.

San Sebastian (the Basque name is Donostia) is the capital of the province of Gipuzkoa. The city is a famous seaside resort town with a population of about 180,000. Heavy industry, commercial fishing, and tourism are the mainstays of the local economy. Vitoria (225,000) is the capital of the province of Araba and also serves as the capital for the entire Basque region. The site of a major battle during the Napoleonic wars, Vitoria today attracts many visitors who flock to its monuments, museums, and cultural festivals.

ARAGON

Long an independent kingdom, Aragon's most famous son was King Ferdinand, who, by marrying Isabella of Castile in 1479, set Spain on the course to world empire. The northern reaches of the region border the Pyrenees and are wooded and well watered, representing a mecca for skiers, hikers, and other outdoor enthusiasts. The southern districts, on the other hand, are quite dry but hold important mineral deposits. The largest city in Aragon is Zaragoza, with a metropolitan population of around 660,000. An industrial center, Zaragoza produces automobiles and processes sugar beets grown in the surrounding countryside. The city was a stronghold of Christianity during the late Roman era. It was taken by Islamic forces in 716, however, and remained part of Muslim Spain for four centuries. Christian forces under the leadership of Alfonso the Battler recaptured the city in 1119, and it soon became the capital of the Christian kingdom of Aragon. Today, the city features many monuments that may be traced to both its Islamic and its Christian masters.

Huesca is the gateway to the Spanish Pyrenees in northern Aragon. Established at least two centuries before the Christian era, the city became a key Roman outpost in Iberia and a vital Muslim fortress during the early Middle Ages. Tourism is the major economic activity here, accommodating the hordes of skiers who appear in winter and the droves of hikers and campers who show up during the summer months. The city also offers some spectacular architecture. Aragon's principle city in the south is Teruel, a city of around 30,000 located in the heart of arid plains and grassy hills. The province that surrounds Teruel has experienced a dramatic decline in population over the last century, and southern Aragon may be characterized as "forgotten Spain." The Spanish government has invested little in this hinterland. The inhabitants suffered mightily during the civil war, as

Barcelona, the capital city of the province of Catalonia, is located on the Mediterranean Sea in eastern Spain. The metropolitan area has more than 4.5 million residents and is the second largest in Spain (behind Madrid). Pictured here are shoppers at one of Barcelona's many markets.

Teruel was the site of heavy fighting between the Republican and Nationalist forces. Today, the area remains one of the poorest in the country.

CATALONIA

Spain's easternmost region (of the mainland) is Catalonia. The heart of the region is the Costa Brava, a stretch of coastline running from the border with France in the north, southward to Spain's second-largest city, Barcelona. This is one of Spain's and the world's great playgrounds, offering beaches, beautiful water, and a vibrant culture and nightlife. Northern Catalonia is marked by magnificent scenery, courtesy of the Pyrenees Mountains. Barcelona, at nearly 4,500,000 people, is Spain's second-most populous city and a hub of economic and cultural life. The industrialization of the city in the nineteenth century led to a steady expansion of its population and margins. At the same time that Barcelona became a focus of Modernism, embodied in the work of famous avant-garde architect Antoni Gaudi and the surrealist painter and sculptor Pablo Picasso. By the early twentieth century, Barcelona had become the center of a revival of Catalan culture. This ongoing movement was led by the conservative politician Francesc Cambó, who attempted to promote Catalan autonomy and the Catalan language.

Modern Barcelona is vibrant and bustling. Like its larger cousin Madrid, the city is home to an expanding immigrant community, primarily from North Africa. Barcelona's importance on the global stage was recognized in its hosting of the 1992 Summer Olympics. Other cities of interest in Catalonia include Tarragona (350,000), an important port, and Girona (80,000), a well-preserved medieval city in northern Catalonia.

VALENCIA

Catalonia's southern neighbor is the region of Valencia, another jewel of Spain's Mediterranean coast. The climate across much of the region is subtropical, and citrus fruits, especially oranges, are a major crop. Just as in Catalonia, the shores of Valencia are dotted with miles of wide beaches and accompanying resorts, which cater to the millions of sun worshipers and partiers who pour into the region every summer. The dominant urban area is the city of Valencia, which, with a population of almost 1.5 million, ranks as Spain's third-largest urban area. Like many of Spain's cities, Valencia was founded by the Romans, occupied for centuries by the Moors (Muslims), and eventually conquered by Christians during the Reconquista. The Spanish hero El Cid ruled the city for several years in the eleventh century, but Valencia was not permanently incorporated into Christian Spain until 1238.

After Spain adopted a democratic government in the late 1970s, Valencia experienced a major rebirth that continues today. The city's population expansion over the last 20 years has led to widespread urban sprawl, and the local government has adopted controversial policies in an attempt to limit this process. The city is famous for Las Fallas, a festival in March during which enormous paper-mache statues are paraded in the city streets and then burned every night for five days.

OFFSHORE SPAIN

Offshore Spain consists of two groups of islands, the Canary and Balearic, and the small enclaves of Ceuta and Melilla on the shore of North Africa. The Canary Islands (the name has no relationship to the bird but rather derives from *canaria*, the Latin word for "dog") are a cluster of seven islands just off Africa's northwestern coast. Tenerife is the capital and largest city. The islands are an official autonomous province of Spain and have representation in the Spanish parliament. Tourism is the primary component of the economy.

The Balearic Islands lie in the Mediterranean Sea, along Spain's eastern coast. There are four principal islands: Majorca (Mallorca), which is the largest, Ibiza (Eivissa), Minorca (Menorca), and Formentera. Collectively, the islands attract millions of tourists each year. Ibiza, in particular, is famous for its nightlife and resorts, whereas Majorca offers a variety of activities and attractions, including the opportunity to hike the low mountains that form a spectacular backdrop to the island's beaches. Both Spanish and Catalan are widely spoken in the Balearic chain.

Ceuta and Melilla are both enclaves located on the northern shore of Morocco. Their political status has been the source of a long-standing dispute between Morocco and Spain. Ceuta, located just across the Strait of Gibraltar from mainland Spain, attracts sizable numbers of tourists and has a larger percentage of Spanish residents that Melilla. The latter is located farther east and contains a population that is largely Arabic-speaking. Both enclaves have representation in the Spanish government, and there is little prospect of either being turned over to Moroccan control.

8

Spain
Looks Ahead

Spain appears to have a very bright future. This is especially true when comparing the country with others worldwide. Although many countries face difficult times, Spain is prospering under good political and economic leadership. Changes in global politics, economics, society, and technology during recent decades have created vast opportunities for those entrepreneurs who are willing to take chances. Few countries have taken better advantage of changing opportunities on a global scale than has Spain. Visitors who are familiar with both the "old" and "new" Spain are astonished with the degree of cultural change that has happened in the country. Traditional lifestyles, a feudal society, and poor government are things of the past. Spain is no longer a European backwater. In a matter of decades, the country has emerged as a modern postindustrial nation of people who see their country as an equal partner to other major players on the global stage.

Economic growth and development should continue to expand. The government seeks to develop white-collar jobs requiring technical expertise and high levels of education. Postindustrial societies depend upon well-educated citizens holding high-paying jobs. These traits contribute to a better overall quality of life, and for most Spaniards, life has never been better. Individual incomes have risen steadily. Literacy has reached 98 percent, one percent higher than in the United States. Life expectancy is 79.5 years, two years longer than the average American can expect to live. By nearly any indicator, Spaniards enjoy a standard of living comparable to people in almost any other developed country.

Although it reaps many benefits, postindustrial cultural development creates challenges that Spain will have to meet. One of them is a wealthy yet aging population. Throughout Europe, demographic issues have created economic and political problems. In order to continue unprecedented economic growth, Spain will have to come to grips with the thorny issue of immigration. Just as in the United States, many low-paying jobs will be filled by immigrants, most of whom will be poor Africans searching for a better life. Foreigners make a tremendous contribution to the economy, but they tend to isolate themselves socially. The cultural landscape of their neighborhoods often resembles the place they came from more than native residential areas of their adopted country. Living and working together in a tightly knit community, many immigrants do not learn Spanish or accept Spanish customs. This makes it very difficult for them to improve their position on the socioeconomic scale.

Consequently, many immigrant neighborhoods suffer from various problems. Eventually, the unequal distribution of wealth and opportunity may contribute to serious social and political troubles. This is most apt to happen when the children of first-generation immigrants reach adulthood. Their roots may be African or Asian, but for all practical purposes, they

Spain's population growth rate stands at 0.15 percent, and like most European nations, its population is projected to drop by 2050. The median age for Spanish citizens is 39.5 years and 14.4 percent of the population is under age 15, including these girls who are celebrating the Abril Feria festival.

share the same views, concerns, and expectations as youth anywhere else. The reality is that economic divisions exist and will continue to exist. To avoid the possibility of widespread riots, such as those experienced throughout France in late 2005, Spain must develop an adequate population policy. Such a policy must serve all its residents and not leave any group feeling disenfranchised.

Another continuing political difficulty for the country is its sharp ethnic and regional differences. Spain, as has been noted on several occasions, is not ethnically homogeneous. Even though regions have been granted some political autonomy, and other improvements made, grating issues still need to be addressed. A major concern is a potential breakup of Spain along ethnic lines into several smaller countries. At a time when Europe is finally uniting, Spain's ethnic dilemma is somewhat of a paradox. Catalonia, the Basque region, or any other province with strong feelings of separatism may eventually gain their independence from Spain. Hopefully, such quests (should they occur) will be conducted peacefully. Ironically, once they would achieve independence, they would soon have to join the European Union, which would result in the loss of complete autonomy. One can only hope that all parties will recognize the possibilities offered by a unified Spain: larger markets, more powerful representation in Europe and the rest of the world, a higher standard of living for all regions, and many other benefits. Europeans have learned a valuable lesson from the former Yugoslavia of what can happen when a country splits apart.

Future generations, however, may prevent the separation of Spain simply by default. The process of globalization is creating a worldwide popular culture-driven generation of people. To them, political and other boundaries will cease to exist as major barriers. Many current issues may simply fade away as relics of the twentieth century. The new generation of Spaniards shows a strong preference for learning English, visiting Miami (Florida), and receiving advanced degrees in France, rather than being reminded of the civil war and Franco's dictatorship. Urban dwellers are concerned with day-to-day issues. They are career oriented and not as concerned with long-term problems that may never be solved.

Spain will remain one of the world's main tourist destinations. For several decades, it has been a popular destination for mass tourism. Recently, however, there has been a shift to more elite tourists and activities, much like those found along the French Riviera. This transformation is attracting huge financial investments to develop what is becoming an upscale tourist infrastructure.

Spain's cities face a crisis in urban planning. As is true in any country with rapidly growing urban centers, Spain must reorganize its urban planning. Madrid, Barcelona, and other urban areas need proper regulation in spatial expansion. Metropolitan centers almost always accept more new residents than they can absorb under existing social and economic conditions. In many locations, conditions have become almost unbearable. Real estate prices equal environmental pollution problems—that is, they are both sky high. Traffic resembles a Los Angeles freeway on a bad day. Most cities continue to grow, however, as people seek better social and economic opportunities and the many amenities that cities can offer. Clearly, the future must be carefully planned if the country and its urban centers are going to continue to prosper.

Today, Spain is a country that has achieved remarkable success within a relatively short time. This progress, however, could be slowed or even reversed without proper planning. Currently, the stars appear to be aligned in Spain's favor. They suggest that Spain will achieve most if not all of its goals. Who knows, the country may even win its long-awaited world soccer championship!

Facts at a Glance

Physical Geography

Location Southwestern Europe, bordering the Bay of Biscay, Mediterranean Sea, North Atlantic Ocean, and Pyrenees Mountains, southwest of France. Shares boundaries with three European countries: Andorra, 39.6 miles (63.7 kilometers), France, 387 miles (623 kilometers), and Portugal, 754 miles (1,214 kilometers); also borders Gibraltar and Morocco (Ceuta and Melilla)

Area Total: 194,885 square miles (504,750 square kilometers)

Climate and Ecosystem Mediterranean (hot, dry summers; mild, wet winters), and temperate (clear, hot summers; more moderate cold winters in interior)

Terrain Large, flat to dissected plateau surrounded by rugged hills; Pyrenees Mountains in northeast

Elevation Extremes Pico de Teide (Tenerife) on Canary Islands reaches 12,198 feet (3,718 meters); the lowest elevation is sea level

Land Use Arable land, 26.07%; permanent crops, 9.87%; other, 64.06% (2001)

Irrigated Land 14,054 miles (36,400 square kilometers) (1998 est.)

Natural Hazards Periodic droughts and resulting fires

Environmental Issues Pollution of the Mediterranean Sea from raw sewage and effluents from the offshore production of oil and gas; water quality and quantity nationwide; air pollution; deforestation; desertification

People

Population 40,341,462 (2005 est.); males, 19,722,264 (2005 est.); females, 20,619,198 (July 2005 est.)

Population Density 78.43 people per square kilometer

Population Growth Rate 0.15%

Net Migration Rate 0.99 migrant(s)/1,000 population (2005 est.)

Fertility Rate 1.28 children born/woman (2005 est.)

Life Expectancy at Birth Total population: 79.52 years; males, 76.18 years; females, 83.08 years (2005 est.)

Median Age 39.51 years

Ethnic Groups Composite of Mediterranean and Nordic types: Castilians, Catalonians, Basques, Gitanos (Gypsies)

Religions Roman Catholic, 94%; Islam, 3%; other, 3%

Literacy (age 15 and over can read and write) Total population, 97.9%; males, 98.7%; females, 97.2% (2003 est.)

Economy

Currency	Euro
GDP Purchasing Power Parity (PPP)	$1.017 trillion (2005 est.)
GDP Per Capita (PPP)	$25,200 (2005 est.)
Labor Force	20.67 million (2005 est.)
Unemployment	10.1% (2005 est.)
Labor Force by Occupation	Agriculture, 5.3%; manufacturing, mining, and construction, 30.1%; services, 64.6% (2004 est.)
Industries	Automobiles, chemicals, clay and refractory products, food and beverages, machine tools, medical equipment, metals and metal manufacturers, pharmaceuticals, ship-building, textiles (including apparel, footwear), tourism
Exports	$194 billion (2005 est.)
Imports	$272 billion (2005 est.)
Leading Trade Partners	*Exports*: France, 19.3%; Germany, 11.7%; Portugal, 9.6%; UK, 9%; Italy, 9%; U.S., 4% (2004); *Imports*: Germany, 16.6%; France, 15.8%; Italy, 8.9%; UK, 6.3%; Netherlands, 4.8% (2004)
Export Commodities	Machinery, motor vehicles, foodstuff, electricity, oil, and natural gas
Import Commodities	Consumer goods, fuels, chemicals, foodstuff, and machinery
Transportation	*Highways:* 413,120 miles (664,852 kilometers)–408,988 miles (658,203 kilometers) paved; *Railroads:* 9,185 miles (14,781 kilometers)–4,796 miles (7,718 kilometers), electrified; *Airports:* 156 (2004); *Waterways:* 655 miles (1,054 kilometers)

Government

Country Name	Long form: Kingdom of Spain; Short form: Spain Local short form: *España*
Capital City	Madrid
Type of Government	Parliamentary monarchy
Head of State	King Juan Carlos
Head of Government	President of the Government and Prime Minister Jose Luis Rodriguez Zapatero
Independence	1492, with the end of reconquista
Administrative Divisions	17 autonomous communities and 2 autonomous cities

Communications

TV Stations	224 (1995)
Phones	(including cellular): 55,074,200 (2003)
Internet Users	9,789,000 (2003)

History at a Glance

Before 10000 First humans inhabit the Iberian Peninsula.

1500 Iberian people arrive.

1000–500 Phoenician and Greek colonies are established.

Second Century Roman dominance over Iberia begins.

A.D.

First Century First evidence of Christianity is found; Christianity becomes an official religion by the rule of Constantine I in fourth century.

Fifth to Eighth Century Germanic Visigoths rule Spain.

711 Muslim forces cross the Strait of Gibraltar, occupying most of Spain for the following seven centuries.

1492 The elimination of the last of the Muslim kingdoms in Spain, the end of the reconquista; Christopher Columbus sails from Spain to discover America—the event marks the beginning of Spain as world power.

1588 Spain loses naval supremacy after the Battle of Trafalgar.

Seventeenth to Nineteenth century Spain further loses influence and territories acquired earlier in Europe and Americas.

1704 Spain loses Gibraltar to the United Kingdom.

1936–1939 Civil war between Republican and Nationalist factions leads to death of 350,000 people.

1939 Francisco Franco emerges as dictator of Spain; his rule lasts for 36 years, until his death in 1975.

1955 United Nations (re)accepts Spain into membership.

1959 Euskadi Ta Askatasuna (ETA) is created.

1961 ETA's terrorist activities begin.

1975 King Juan Carlos becomes ruler of Spain after Francisco Franco's death.

1977 Democratic elections return.

1982 Spain joins North Atlantic Treaty Alliance (NATO).

1986	Spain becomes a member of the European Economic Community (EEC), the forerunner to today's European Union (EU).
1992	Barcelona hosts Summer Olympics.
2002	Euro officially replaces peseta as Spanish currency.
2004	The largest terrorist attack in Spanish history takes lives of 192 persons in Madrid bombings.
2005	Spanish voters overwhelmingly support EU Constitution in national referendum.

Bibliography and Further Reading

Books

Frankland, E. Gene. *Global Studies: Europe.* Guilford, CT: Dushkin/McGraw-Hill, 2002.

Jordan-Bychkov, T., and Bella Bychkova-Jordan. *The European Culture Area.* New York: Rowman and Littlefield, 2001.

Kern, Robert W. *The Regions of Spain: A Reference Guide to History and Culture.* Westport, CT: Greenwood Press, 1995.

Pierson, Peter. *The History of Spain.* Westport, CT: Greenwood Press, 1999.

Smith, Catherine-Delano. *Western Mediterranean Europe: A Historical Geography of Italy, Spain, and Southern France since the Neolithic.* New York: Academic Press, 1979.

Stanton, Edward F. *Culture and Customs of Spain.* Westport, CT: Greenwood Press, 2002.

The Economist. "The Second Transition: A Survey of Spain." June 24, 2004, 3-14.

U.S. Department of State. Background Note: Spain. Available at *http://www.state.gov/r/pa/ei/bgn/2878.htm*

Web sites

Online encyclopedia entry on Spain
http://en.wikipedia.org/wiki/Spain

A Country Study: Spain
http://lcweb2.loc.gov/frd/cs/estoc.html

Central Intelligence Agency, World Factbook: Spain.
http://www.odci.gov/cia/publications/factbook/geos/sp.html

Information on Spanish current affairs and its historical, linguistic, and cultural development
http://www.sispain.org/

Spain Tourism
http://www.spain.info/

Index

Index

Index

Picture Credits

page:

11: Zuma Press/NMI
14: New Millennium Images
21: © Lucidity Information Design
24: © Lucidity Information Design
27: KRT/NMI
32: Miguel Riopa/AFP/
    Getty Images/NMI
36: New Millennium Images
42: Associated Press, AP

48: New Millennium Images
52: Associated Press, AP/EFE
55: Associated Press, AP/EFE
61: Associated Press, AP
66: Associated Press, AP
70: Associated Press, AP
77: Zuma Press/NMI
83: AFP/NMI
89: Zuma Press/NMI

Cover: New Millennium Images

About the Contributors

ZORAN "ZOK" PAVLOVIĆ is a cultural geographer currently working at Oklahoma State University in Stillwater. *Spain* is Zok's eighth book authored or coauthored for the Chelsea House geography series MODERN WORLD NATIONS. He also authored *Europe* for the MODERN WORLD CULTURES series. In geography his interests are culture theory, evolution of geographic thought, and geography of viticulture. He was born and raised in southeastern Europe.

REUEL R. HANKS is Associate Professor of Geography at Oklahoma State University in Stillwater. Hanks specializes in economic and political geography and is the author of two reference books, *Central Asia: A Global Studies Handbook* and *Uzbekistan: World Bibliographical Series*, and several articles and book chapters on Central Asia.

CHARLES F. GRITZNER is Distinguished Professor of Geography at South Dakota State University in Brookings. He is now in his fifth decade of college teaching, scholarly research, and writing. In addition to teaching, he enjoys traveling, writing, working with teachers, and sharing his love of geography with students and readers alike. As Consulting Editor and frequent author for the Chelsea House MODERN WORLD NATIONS and MODERN WORLD CULTURES series, he has a wonderful opportunity to combine each of these "hobbies."

Professionally, Gritzner has served as both President and Executive Director of the National Council for Geographic Education. He has received numerous awards in recognition of his academic and teaching achievements, including the NCGE's George J. Miller Award for Distinguished Service to geography and geographic education and the American Association of Geographers' award for Excellence in Teaching.